THE BOOK OF
DRAFT
HORSES

THE GENTLE GIANTS THAT
BUILT THE WORLD

Written By

DONNA CAMPBELL SMITH

Photographs By

DONNA CAMPBELL SMITH

THE LYONS PRESS
Guilford, Connecticut

An imprint of The Globe Pequot Press

The Lyons Press is an imprint of The Globe Pequot Press.

10 9 8 7 6 5 4 3 2 1

Printed in the United States of America

ISBN 978-1-59228-979-0

Library of Congress Cataloging-in-Publication Data is available on file.

DEDICATION

I dedicate this book to the memory of Dan and Maude. I never met them in real life; but Daddy told me stories about them, Dan in particular. Dan and Maude were workhorses. They belonged to my Grandpa Campbell, who used them on the farm during the week, then hitched one or both to the wagon on Saturdays to take the family into town. Daddy and his sister, Myrtle, also rode them for fun. Dan and Maude were the quintessential family farm horses.

Ole Dan evidently felt a sense of ownership for Daddy, and I know Daddy was especially fond of him. Aunt Myrtle's favorite was Maude, and her family photo album contains pictures of her riding and doing tricks on Maude's wide back. Each horse and each child enjoyed a special relationship.

My cousin Dave remembers hearing how Grandpa Campbell would carry his lunch to work in the fields in his overalls pocket, and whenever Dan got the chance he'd steal Grandpa's lunch right out of his pocket. I have to believe my grandfather got a kick out of that, or he wouldn't have let a horse get away with such shenanigans.

Whenever the family started telling horse tales, Daddy would tell the one about the Christmas he got a shiny, new red bobsled. According to Daddy, Dan became jealous of that sled. As far as Dan was concerned, that sled was just getting way too much attention. One day Daddy left the sled unattended in Dan's pasture. When he remembered and came back to get it, he was too late. He arrived just in time to see Dan very purposefully walk over to the sled and stomp it to smithereens.

Daddy always laughed when he told that story. Then, often as not, he'd get quiet and a little sad, and tell us Ole Dan died of nightshade poisoning, or so they thought. "That Dan, he was a good horse," Daddy would say and then shake his head as if to clear his mind of the sad memory.

So, to Dan and Maude, and all the "work" horses that have blessed their families with fond memories, I dedicate this book to you.

Aunt Myrtle riding Dan or Maude.

TABLE OF CONTENTS

ACKNOWLEDGMENTS

Writing this book and photographing the horses for it has been a delightful experience. People have let me come to their farms and given of their time and expertise, while treating me like an old friend. Perfect strangers have let me photograph their horses and interview them for this book. I am especially thankful to Mr. Jimmy Dozier for extending to me true southern hospitality at the plow day held on his farm, and to Frankie Faithful for sharing his horses and knowledge with me. Mr. C.B. Daughtridge gave hours of his time to show me around his beautiful farm and let me photograph his spotted draft horses. JR and Roxanne Thrower also extended their hospitality to me and let me photograph their beautiful Shire horses. Thank you, Lisa Miller, Debra Moorman, Barry and Clara Leonard, Tom and Pam Vybiral, Lynn Johnson, Rebecca Cannon, Becky Beach, and Amy Snyder for letting me meet and photograph your horses. Kim Jones, thank you for your support. A special thank you to Al Boykin for introducing me to draft horse owners all over North Carolina and for sharing your knowledge.

Many people have helped me through the Internet, and even though we've not met in person, it feels like we have. Jason Rutledge, Neil Dimmock, Denise Pullis, and many others took time out to answer my questions and share photos of their horses at work—thank you.

Steven D. Price, my editor, and The Lyons Press, I thank for giving me a second go; and Rita Rosenkranz, my agent, for expertly taking care of business.

Family and friends, I know you get tired of hearing me go on about my writing projects. Thank you for not saying so.

CHAPTER ONE

HISTORY OF THE DRAFT HORSE

WHILE THE ANCIENT EGYPTIANS DOMESTICATED HORSES and used them for driving and as beasts of burden, the first use of horses was for food. Archeologists have found mounds of bones from butchered horse carcasses around the camps of Paleolithic people. It is also believed mares were kept for milking in those ancient times. It took a long time for human ingenuity to see the horse as much more than a food source. Once that realization dawned, there seemed to be no end to how we could enlist the help of the horse to make life easier for us. It was the heavy horse, the draft horse that seemed most suited for helping with the advancement of civilized man.

The largest of the modern horse, the draft horse can trace its heritage to the European wild horse known as the Black Horse of Flanders. This draft-type horse, larger and blockier than the swift horses of the Orient, was native to Western Europe about the time of the Roman Invasion in AD 43. These horses flourished in the rich, fertile valleys and flood plains of Europe. Through selective breeding, people in various areas developed types to suit their needs, and these were the forerunners of today's draft horse breeds.

The medieval horses, know as Great Horses, were used in a not-so-civilized manner as war machines. The draft, or heavy, horse was found to be indispensable as a mount for knights. The weight of a knight wearing his armor was over four hundred pounds, an unfair burden for the light horses from the East.

The gear of the horse consisted of saddle, bridle, and a drape across its rear. Armor to protect the head, neck, and chest was made of overlapping plates that were laced together. The plates were made

Museum display of an armored horse and knight of the European middle ages, Zwinger Museum, Dresden.
Photographer: Ingersoll

of a variety of materials including hard leather, horn or bone, and sometimes iron. Chain mail was put between quilted layers of cloth, or the chain mail was simply laid under the cloth. The fabric was tapestry or brocade and sometimes highly decorated. Colors and patterns on the girth and breast collar indicated rank. Tassels were used to decorate the horse's head and neck. Sometimes the horse was attired in plain leather trappings. The bridle had two sets of reins, one made of leather and the other chain wrapped in leather. The fancy armor was used in ceremonies and tournaments, with less ornate armor used in battle.

Likewise, the knight's armor was made of chain mail, metal plates, or leather breastplates stuffed with straw.

The combined weight of warrior and horse was in and of itself a weapon used to batter foes—very effectively—as two thousand or more pounds bore down to smash into soldiers and run them through with lances. Leonardo da Vinci and other artists depict the monstrous warhorses as fierce killing machines, with eyes flashing, ears pinned, and teeth bared. That picture is a far cry from today's impression of the draft as a gentle giant.

The War Horse was called a *destrier*, meaning "in the right hand." The term comes from the fact that the knight's squire led the war horse to the battle field, while the knight rode a lighter, smoother gaited horse en route in order to save the destrier's stamina for the battle. The reins were held in the left hand, leaving the squire's right hand free to hold a sword or lance. The most desired characteristics of the destrier were strength, speed, and agility. War Horses were expensive, and nobles used the horses as payment to the soldiers who fought their wars. The Rolls Royce of War Horses were called coursers. They were the most expensive of all, demanding sometimes ten times the price of the ordinary destrier.

When the heavy horses were not being used in battle, they provided sport and entertainment for the masses in tournaments. Tournaments, or melees, were mock battles, although they still ended in bloodshed and death. The name tournament comes from the Latin word *tornare*, meaning "to turn," referring to the fast turns the horses had to make in the melees as two teams played against each other. They had flags on their backs, and the object was to remove the opponent's flags using clubs and swords.

During the 12th century, the church outlawed the tournaments, but the contests continued, with blunt weapons being used in place of the real thing, but they still involved violent contact, and often resulted in the death of some participants. The tournament was a huge affair. Royalty from visiting countries joined the hosting nobility on a grandstand built up high so they all could look down on the activities. Banners and flags with the spectators' coats of arms decorated the grandstand. Ladies gave their favorite knight a glove or handkerchief to let him know they favored him. The common people watched from ground level under tents.

The following excerpts from *The Brut or The Chronicles of England*, (translation by Steven Muhlberger) describes the atmosphere of a tournament held in 1388:

> *In this aforesaid parliament, in the twelfth year of King Richard's reign, he had cried and proclaimed general jousts, what is usually called a tournament, of lords, knights and squires. And these jousts or tournaments were held in London at Smithfield, for all manner of foreigners, whatever land or country they might come from, and they were made very welcome; and for them and everyone else it was open house, and there were great feasts held. And also great gifts were given to all manner of foreigners. And those on the king's side wore a uniform: on their coats, armor, shields, horses and trappings were white harts, with a crown around their necks, and chains of gold hanging thereupon, and the crown hanging low upon the hart's body. This hart was the king's livery which he gave to lords and ladies, knights and squires, so his household could be distinguished from other people. And at the opening of the*

jousts, twenty-four ladies led twenty-four lords of the Garter with chains of gold, and all were in the same livery of harts described before, leading the lords on horseback from the Tower through the city of London to Smithfield, where the jousts were to be done. And this feast and joust was open to all who wished to come, of whatever land or nation they might be. And it was held over twenty-four days, at the king's own cost. These twenty-four lords requited anyone who wished to come there. And the Count of St. Pol from France came, and with him many other worthy knights from diverse places, all well arrayed. And out of Holland and Hainault came the Lord of Ostrevant, that was the son of the Duke of Holland, and many other worthy knights with him, both of Holland and Hainault, well arrayed. And when these feasts and jousts were accomplished and came to an end, the king thanked these strangers and gave them many great gifts; and then they took their leave of the king and the other lords and ladies, and went home again to their own country, with great love and much gratitude.

This writing shows how the tournaments were important politically, as well as entertaining.

To be eligible to enter the games, the knight or squire had to have a suit of armor, a sword and shield, and a horse. These items were expensive and the stakes were high since a losing or cheating knight had to forfeit his horse to his opposition.

At the end of the tournament knights often challenged one another to a joust, which often ended in the death of the loser as described in another passage from *The Brut or The Chronicles of England:*

And in the seventeenth year of his [Richard II's] reign, certain lords of Scotland came to England to win renown through deeds of arms. And these are the persons: The Earl of Mar, who challenged the Earl Marshal of England to joust with him certain points on horseback with sharp spears. And so they rode against each other certain courses, like two worthy knights and lords, but not the full challenge that the Scottish earl made. For he was cast down, both horse and man, and two of his ribs were broken in the fall; and so he was carried out of Smithfield and home to his inn. And a little time afterwards he was carried homeward in a litter, and at York he died.

By the 16th century the tournament became more a festival, with a great deal of pageantry. The joust was the highlight of the festival. Jousting matches were both team and individual contests. A panel of judges awarded prizes for various "classes," such as who stayed in the longest without losing his helmet, who struck the best blow, and who broke the most lances in a day. The prizes were presented with a kiss. Dancing and feasting were all part of the festival.

By the 17th century, the tournaments had become a lot like our horse shows and gymkhanas, with displays of horsemanship. A contest called "the running of the rings" in which the horseman speared rings on his lance, replaced jousting.

It was much later before horses were used for farming. The common man could not afford a horse. Horses were for the rich. Villagers did farming with a communal system, sharing land, plows, horses and oxen, and the harvest. It was the feudal system that made farming with horses possible, since the Lord of the Manor could afford horses for the farmers to use in tilling the land. Horses made commerce between cities and countries more profitable, since they could pull heavy loads of goods and transport man and goods with relative speed. So, the horse not only became a symbol of wealth, but also of independence.

As time went on, draft horse breeds were developed throughout the Old World to suit the needs of the people. Farming changed as individuals were able to own land, and the horse became an indispensable means of bringing crops to harvest and providing profit.

DRAFT HORSES IN AMERICA

Colonial horses were mostly light horse breeds descended from Spanish horses brought over by early explorers. Once land was cleared and crops grown, mules and oxen were the dominant draft animals. Heavy horses were not needed for farming and wagon pulling until the westward movement in the 18th century. In the 1730s, the Conestoga Horse was developed in Eastern Pennsylvania specifically to pull freight wagons and to double as saddle horses. They were the result of mixed breeding, mainly Flemish stallions and colonial mares. Another draft type was the Vermont Drafter. These early draft types helped clear the land for farmers, skidding logs expertly and hauling sleds loaded with tree trunks to the sawmills.

In the postwar period of the late 1800s, urban growth and industry called for a way to transport goods by wagonloads. Draft horses were used to move those goods from trains and boats to the interior of the country. Cities grew, and the concept of mass transit gave the big horses more jobs to do. Horse-drawn buses transported people on street railways in more than 300 American cities during that time. This continued until the late 19th century and early 20th century when the automobile replaced most of the horse-powered trucks and buses.

The mining industry also used draft horse teams to transport wagons loaded with tons of ore, coal, and other minerals from the mines to the railroads. The famous Twenty-Mule Team used by the Pacific Coast Borax Company did indeed use mules, but draft horses often filled the wheel position (that directly in front of the wagon) because of their size and strength.

In 1825 the Erie Canal opened trade routes from the Hudson River to Lake Erie. Barges loaded with people and goods were driven by horsepower—draft horse and mule power. The horses pulled the barges through the water in the canals by walking along dirt towpaths beside the canal. They traveled about four miles an hour. The tons of cargo the barges could haul made up for the slow time.

FIRE HORSES

Draft horses were also used by fire stations from the mid-1860s until the early 1900s to pull heavy equipment wagons. Horses were needed to pull steam powered pump wagons, the water carried in tanks on the wagons, and heavy wooden ladders. Chemical engines came into use during the 1870s. Chemical engines acted like big fire extinguishers when a small bottle of sulfuric acid and large tanks of water were mixed with bicarbonate of soda. The reaction was more efficient than water alone.

The horses had to be fearless, as well as strong and fast. They were stabled in the firehouse, along with the firefighting equipment. The firemen on watch slept upstairs. The harnesses were hung just over the horses. When the alarm rang a lever was pulled that dropped the harness in place onto the horses. The firemen could then quickly hitch the horses to the wagons.

Different bell tones indicated the fire's location. There are stories that the excited horses sometimes took off for the fire, leaving the firemen behind. The more experienced horses learned the bell code, and such runaways are said to have arrived at the fire without the firemen.

A good firefighting team had to be able to work together, matching stride for stride. A fire team's color was not important. A team of mix-matched colors is called a Boston Match, the term originating with Boston's fire horses. The term is still used for a team of horses of unmatched colors.

Sometimes cities sent their horses to fire-fighting schools. The horse's education didn't stop upon graduation, though. Horses were

A Boston Match is a team of horses whose colors do not match.

drilled daily. In some cities they were hitched and drilled three times a day. Care and feeding were strictly monitored. Only the most reliable firefighters were allowed to care for the horses.

Fire horses race to the scene.

Farm Horses

As agriculture underwent the metamorphosis from family farming to business farming, there was a need for a draft animal that could work faster than oxen. Draft stallions were imported from Europe, and there was a draft horse boom in the United States. The Kellogg Stock Farm of Green Bay, Wisconsin, advertised Percheron stallions imported from France in a 19th-century sales flyer. The flyer quoted Professor W.A. Henry of the University of Wisconsin: "The average farmer gets the whole advantage of blooded stock in the use of the full blooded male crossed with the common native stock." So, the Percheron stallions were sold to farmers to upgrade their mixed breed mares.

As technology in farming advanced and equipment became larger and heavier, the demand for draft horses increased. The one-horse plow gave way to huge cultivators and combines pulled by teams. One farm could tend much larger acreage. By the dawn of the 20th century there were thousands of draft horses in the United States tending thousands of acres of land. Human ingenuity found countless ways for horses to lighten the workload on the farm. Horses powered threshing machines and cotton gins, and other machines were invented. One way horses were used to separate grain from shaft was the two-story stomping barn. The wheat was spread out on the second floor. Horses were led up a steep ramp and then walked in circles on the wheat, causing the grain to drop through cracks in the floor to the bottom level. Smaller horses worked better for this job, although big feet were certainly a plus.

Westward Movement

The westward movement opened another market for draft horses. In the Conestoga Valley of Lancaster County, Pennsylvania in the early

Horses walk a treadmill that operates a cotton gin during a colonial re-enactment at the Old Threshers Reunion, Denton, NC.

1700s, Mennonite German settlers developed a horse designed particularly for pulling the Conestoga wagon. Four-to-six horse teams hauled these wagons westward. The deep-bodied wagon came to be known as the Prairie Schooner because of its resemblance to a boat. The Conestoga Horse is thought to have first resulted from crossing three Flemish stallions imported by William Penn with Virginia's colonial mares. Other breeds were later mixed in, and truthfully the Conestoga was more a type than a breed. Most of the horses were black, stood about 16.2 to 17 hands, and weighed up to 1,800 pounds. The legs were not feathered; they were well muscled and had a long, ground-covering stride. They were required to move heavy loads long distances over dangerous terrain.

The Conestoga Horses were used to carry materials to build railroads, move families west, and pull stagecoaches. As farms and towns sprang up in the west, the Conestoga fulfilled many roles. Sadly, as need for workhorses diminished, the Conestoga died out by the early 1900s.

MODERN WAR HORSE

By the early 1900s American draft horse breeding was big business, with thousands of horses being exported to European countries, a turnaround from the previous century. The reason for this was that the First World War created a demand for draft horses to pull artillery and supplies to the front lines. Many of the warhorses were killed in battles throughout Europe. Of 182,000 horses sent from the United States, only 200 returned.

On October 15, 1921, the American Red Star Animal Relief unveiled a bronze tablet at the State, War, and Navy Building in Washington, DC, to honor the horses and mules that died during the First World War. General Willard A. Holbrook, former Chief of Cavalry, made an acceptance speech for the United States Government. In the beginning of his speech General Holbrook said, "Through the ages of conflict and strife the horse has been the constant companion and steadfast friend of the soldier, sharing his suffering and dangers, his toil and hardship and consecrating the battlefield with his blood."

He concluded his speech with these words: "This imperishable bronze will ever bear silent witness of the great debt we owe our equine friend, and will inspire in the hearts of the present and future generations a determination to see that they receive the treatment and consideration which is their due."

DRAFT HORSE DECLINE

After the war the market for draft horses was practically extinct in America. The army no longer needed them. The draft horse heyday in the cities came to a screeching halt by the 1920s as gasoline-powered vehicles replaced the horses for public transportation and transporting goods. According to an article at www.easterndrafthorse.com titled "Draft Horses in America," the last vehicles to give way from horse-drawn to gasoline-driven in the 1930s were the horse-drawn hearses. The draft horse was even being replaced on farms by tractors. Registered draft horses numbered only 2,000 by 1945. By the 1950s, some registries had closed their offices.

COMEBACK

Fortunately, a resurgence of interest in the draft horse occurred in the 1970s, maybe as a result of gas shortages and high prices at the pump. Small farmers turned back to the original horsepower. Registration of new foals climbed. Draft horses today are showing up on small farms, in the logging industry, in the show ring and pulling competitions, and in the back yard as pleasure horses. The big hitches are making it big in advertising and exhibitions, and the draft crossbred has grown in popularity by leaps and bounds, particularly in the sport horse industry. Their steady disposition also makes them ideal school and therapy horses. The draft horse's spot in American history seems to be secure.

CHAPTER TWO

DRAFT HORSE BREEDS

THERE ARE SEVERAL DRAFT HORSE BREEDS, EACH WITH ITS own unique qualities that fit them for a particular job or appearance. They all have the same roots, the Black Horse of Flanders. We have five major breeds in the United States: Belgian, Clydesdale, Shire, Suffolk Punch, and Percheron. In addition to those are several minor breeds and draft ponies. The ponies measure fewer than 14.2 hands high, but share all the other qualities of the draft horse, including strength, stamina, and even temperament.

PRIMARY BREEDS

Belgian Draft Horse

The Belgian shares its very beginnings with that of most heavy horse breeds: the great horse of medieval times. The breeders of Belgium developed a heavy horse to meet their needs. This Western European country had all the conditions necessary for abundant farm production, and they needed a horse that could help farm this land.

Farmers in surrounding countries coveted the horses of Belgium. Breeders were blessed with an extended market for their horses and began to export stallions. The government of Belgium encouraged the Belgian horse business by establishing a series of district shows and the National Show in Brussels to show the world what they had. The government also set up an inspection committee for stallions to ensure quality control and to establish a set breed type. By 1891 Belgium was exporting Belgian horses to government stables throughout Europe.

Three main bloodlines were developed by that time. The Gros de la Dendre lines trace from the stallion Orange 1. Most bay Belgians are from this line. The Gris du Hainaut line traces to the stallion Bayard. They are gray, dun, sorrel, and red roan. A line stemming from Jean 1 through a stallion named Colosses de la Mehaique is known for incredible strength. Never having been crossed with light horses, the Belgian has maintained its purity as a breed and still resembles the Flanders horse of the Middle Ages.

In 1886 Dr. A.G. Van Hoorebeke of Monmouth, Illinois, imported the first Belgians to the United States. The American Association of Importers and Breeders of Belgian Draft Horses was established in February 1887. The name was later changed to Belgian Draft Corporation of America. The headquarters is now in Wabash, Indiana. But it was after the 1903 World Fair in St. Louis that Americans took a real interest in Belgian horses. The Belgium government sent Belgians to that expo and the International Livestock Expo in Chicago. By 1910 almost 2000 Belgian had been registered in North America.

World War I in 1914 closed importation of horses, and Americans began their own breeding program in earnest. They began to make some changes in the horse to fit their needs, resulting in what is called the American Style Belgian. A more refined head and more sloping shoulder made the American Belgian a fancier looking and moving horse. The American breeders faulted the old Belgian for having a too small and round hoof for its massive body and through selective breeding improved the Belgian's foot.

As with other draft breeds, the number of Belgians in American declined after World War II. The number of horses registered in the early 1950s was only a couple of hundred a year. The association persevered through the lean years. Slowly, the draft horse industry made a comeback. Prices rose until the 1980s, when the number of Belgian horses surpassed its heyday of the 1930s to become one of the most popular draft horses in America.

The typical Belgian Draft Horse today is chestnut with a flaxen mane and tail, but can also be the more rare roan, black, gray, or brown. They are the most massive of the draft breeds, known for their draftiness, built deep through the heart girth and wide in the chest. They stand from 15.2 to 17 hands high and weigh anywhere from 1,900 to 2,200 pounds. The American Belgian is more refined through the head and neck and cleaner legged than their European cousin the Brabant, a thicker bodied and draftier horse with feathered legs. The American Brabant Association preserves this old style Belgian, whose most common colors are bay and bay roan.

The Belgian's sheer massiveness and power, coupled with their patient and docile personality, make them a natural in pulling competitions. They also excel in the show ring, are popular hitch horses, and can be found working as farm and ranch horses all over the country.

**Belgian teammates, Marty and Mary, owned by Jimmy Dozier
of Rocky Mount, NC.**

Clydesdale

The Clydesdale may be the best-known draft horse among America's general population. This horse is famous for pulling the Budweiser Beer Wagon and stars in some of the Super Bowl's most memorable commercials. What other breed can play football?

The origin of the Clydesdale is in southern Scotland, where it was first developed in the early 1800s by farmers in the region of Clydesdale, which is now known as Lanarkshire. Legend has it that the Duke of Hamilton imported six black Flemish coach stallions from Flanders. These horses were bred to domestic mares and eventually resulted in the Clydesdale.

While farming was the primary use of the first Clydesdales, the breed soon became an important contributor to the mining industry of the land. The horse's reputation as a tractable, strong, and agile workhorse spread easily from Scotland to England, and by the late part of the century the horses were being exported to the United States and Canada.

As with other workhorses in the United States, the Clydesdale followed a dip in numbers with the onset of mechanization. It has gained in popularity in the 20th century in the show arena and in work. The breed is a popular carriage and riding horse. There are about 4,000 Clydesdales registered in America today.

Some physical characteristics that set the Clydesdale apart from other draft horses are the long, white feathering on its legs, bold white facial and leg markings, its high leg action, and high head carriage. Most are bays, but they can also be black, brown, or chestnut and even spotted or roan. Color is not a consideration in the show ring, but the most popular hitch horses are usually bay with a blaze and four white stockings or socks.

Clydesdales stand from 16 to 19 hands and weigh from 1,600 to 2,200 pounds. The breed is well known for being sound, with a good size foot and strong legs. The over-all conformation creates a balanced, agile horse with substance. Size should never outweigh good conformation. A long, ground-covering stride and high leg action are desired, and of course a Clydesdale is expected to have a willing disposition and intelligence.

Anheuser-Busch owns 225 to 250 Clydesdale Horses, making them the largest breeder of Clydesdales in the world. The Budweiser Clydesdales are also the most traveled horses in the world, logging 100,000 miles per year to appear in parades, festivals, rodeos, horse shows, and other events. The company has five eight-horse hitches that travel all over North America and sometimes overseas. The horses can also be seen at the Anheuser-Busch farm in St. Louis and the Anheuser-Busch Theme parks in Williamsburg, Virginia; Orlando, Florida; San Diego, California; and San Antonio, Texas.

The antique wagons pulled by the Budweiser Clydesdales are 1903 Studebaker-built beer wagons that have been carefully restored and painted in red, white, and gold. The harnesses weigh 130 pounds each with custom-fit collars.

Budweiser Clydesdale Team delivers beer to the White House.
Courtesy of Anheuser-Busch Companies, Inc.

The Anheuser-Busch Budweiser horses became a tradition in 1933 after August Busch Jr. gave his father a team of six geldings to celebrate the end of prohibition. Seeing the beer wagon as an ideal promotional vehicle, Mr. Busch sent the team by rail to New York City. There they picked up two cases of beer at the New Jersey Newark Airport. The team first delivered a case of beer to the New York governor, Al Smith, who had been instrumental in repealing prohibition. From there the Clydesdales traveled throughout the New England and mid-Atlantic states, going from city to city by rail. The hitch also delivered a case of beer to President Franklin Delano Roosevelt at the White House. This was the birth of one of the best advertising campaigns in business history.

In addition to their fame in the advertising world, Clydesdale horses are also popular in the show ring. The National Clydesdale Horse Show has run for over thirty years and offers halter classes, junior exhibitor showmanship, and various carts and hitch classes. The Clydesdale can also be found competing in events outside its

**Clydesdale Stallion, Top Gun Commander McDuff,
owned by Barry and Clara Leonard of Lexington, NC.**

breed shows. They are popular riding horses, both as pleasure horses and for competing in hunter, jumping, and dressage shows.

Percheron

Known as the breed of blacks and grays, the true origin of the Percheron is debatable. Some take it back to the Ice Age, while other historians trace them to the Boulonnais of the Roman Invasion. Another common theory is that they descended from the Oriental horses of the Moors. The most common deduction is that in the Middle Ages in a province of France called Le Perche, Arabian and Andalusian horses were crossed with the native mares of Le Perche to produce the Percheron horse. It is possible that all of those horses made a contribution to what became known as the Percheron Horse.

The people of Le Perche, which is about 50 miles southwest of Paris, France, have a long history of breeding and selling horses. The area has the requirements needed for raising livestock: plenty of water and fertile pastureland. Their horses became well known and sought after by the people of surrounding countries, who imported the horses to improve their own stock.

The Percherons were first bred for war mounts, carrying the heavily armored knights into battle. The invention of firearms changed warfare, and the requirements changed from heavy horses to speedier light horses. The breeders adapted and bred the heavy horse for pulling coaches called diligences, and these horses became known as Diligence Horses. The color gray was preferred because gray horses were easier to see when goods were being transported at night. With gray being a dominant color, probably from the Arab and Andalusian bloodlines, the Percheron filled that requirement.

In the 18th century, Arabian and Thoroughbred stallions were crossed with Percheron mares. Today all Percherons can be traced to one of those stallions in particular, Jean Le Blanc.

Easing into a more modern era, a still heavier horse was developed for public transport in cities. Later, with the advent of the rail

THE KELLOGG STOCK FARM,

OF GREEN BAY, WISCONSIN,

has imported from France several fine Percheron Stallions, which are now within the easy reach of the Farmers of Brown, Manitowoc, Kewaunee, Chippewa and Eau Claire Counties. Any farmer, who now owns one of our colts, wants more of them. Is this a mere fancy, because people usually think "their own geese to be swans?" We think not. A few figures will show why pure-bred stallions ought to get better colts, by far, than graded stallions.

RULE FOR CALCULATING THE AMOUNT OF PURE BLOOD IN A COLT.

Add the pure blood of the sire to the pure blood of the dam, and divide the sum by two, and the result will give the pure blood of the colt.

In the first example, the colt, in each case, is supposed to be bred to a pure-bred horse. The pure-blooded horse is indicated by 1, and the native mare by 0.

FIRST CROSS	..1 added to	0,	divided by 2,	equals	1-2.
SECOND "	..1 "	1-2,	"	2,	"	3-4.
THIRD "	..1 "	3-4,	"	2,	"	7-8.
FOURTH "	..1 "	7-8,	"	2,	"	15-16.
FIFTH "	..1 "	15-16,	"	2,	"	31-32.

The fifth cross with a full-blooded horse entitles the owner *to register his colt as a pure-bred.*

CROSSES OF A NATIVE MARE WITH A HALF-BRED STALLION.

FIRST CROSS	..1-2 added to	0,	divided by 2,	equals	1-4.
SECOND "	..1-2 "	1-4,	"	2,	"	3-8.
THIRD "	..1-2 "	3-8,	"	2,	"	7-16.
FOURTH "	..1-2 "	7-16,	"	2,	"	15-32.
FIFTH "	..1-2 "	15-32,	"	2,	"	31-64.

Crosses of a native mare with a half-blood stallion, if continued indefinitely, *can never quite reach a half-blood.*

From these figures it is plain that more pure blood results from one cross with our pure-bred stock than from ten, one hundred or even one thousand crosses with a half-breed. It is an old saying that "Blood will tell," which is particularly true in horses.

Professor W. A. Henry, of the Agricultural Department of the University of Wisconsin, has given the Wisconsin farmers much valuable advice; valuable, because always disinterested. (He has nothing to sell.) The following extracts are from his address before the Northern Wisconsin Agricultural Society:

"I make this statement, knowing it is to be put in print, and wish it could be read by every thoughtful farmer in Wisconsin:"

(1) "In my judgment, grades are better for farmers, for practical purposes, than full bloods."

(2) "The rock, on which our farmers split, is this: finding out that a grade animal is as good for practical purposes, they reason that he must be as good as a full blood for breeding purposes, *which is a fatal mistake.*"

(3) "Here is the pith of the whole lecture: *The average farmer gets the whole advantage of blooded stock in the use of the full blooded male, crossed with the common native stock.*"

At first thought, the farmer will say, "Twenty-five dollars for a living colt, or fifteen dollars for the season, is too much." "I can't afford it." In one sense this is true and in another it is a mistake. The charge for graded stallions is commonly $10; for some much less. One man in Kewaunee County will breed a mare (if the farmer refuses to pay more) for half a bushel of potatoes. Our charge *does* seem high compared with this. On the other hand a first-class imported Percheron stallion costs $2,500, of which one per cent. is $25, while a half-bred commonly costs $400, of which one per cent. is $4. It should be remembered that warranting *a living colt* is quite another thing from warranting a mare *in foal.* Any owner of a first-class Percheron stallion in Illinois would laugh at the farmer who asked him to warrant a living colt for $25.

Again, what does $5 or $10 amount to compared with the difference between the price of a first-rate three-year old colt and one only of medium quality?

WISCONSIN FARMERS! You are ten or fifteen years behind the farmers of Illinois and Iowa in breeding draft horses. Talk with your friends in those states and you will find that we are telling you the truth.

Kellogg Stock Farm advertises pure Percheron Stallions in the late 19th century.

system, the strong horses were used to pull loads of crops to ship docks and rail stations. Strong horses were also in demand by farmers. The breeders of Le Perche continued to adapt the horses to meet the needs of their buyers.

The United States first imported draft horses from France in the mid-1800s, not from Le Perche, but from Normandy. During the 1870s through the 1880s, thousands of draft horses, mostly stallions, were brought to the United States from France and Great Britain. The most superior horses were found at Le Perche.

The National Association of Importers and Breeders of Norman Horses was established in Chicago in 1875. Later the name of the association was changed to Percheron-Norman Horses. By the 1880s the horses had gained in popularity, and about 5,000 stallions and 2,500 mares were imported from France.

One of those breeders was Rufus Bela Kellogg, who was born in Massachusetts in 1837. He was a banker and moved to Wisconsin in 1873 and founded Kellogg National Bank. When he retired from banking he established a stock farm and became well known for his purebred Percheron horses. He imported stallions and promoted them as a way to improve native stock, in addition to breeding and selling purebreds.

In 1893 an economic crisis in the Unites States brought the importations to a temporary halt. Purchases resumed in 1898, with the Percheron making a huge comeback. Ten thousand horses were registered per year through the early part of the 20th century. In 1902 a new breed association was formed, picking up the old pedigree records.

World War I brought another halt to importing draft horses and an increase in American-bred horses. Automation was beginning to replace "horse power" in the cities. The Great Depression was actually good for the draft horse population. Horses were still being used on the farms, since gasoline was hard to come by in rural areas.

Percherons were the favored breed, making up 70 percent of the draft horses in America in the 1930s. In 1937 registration reached 4,611, and imports increased again.

World War II had an opposite effect on the population of the workhorses. Gasoline was plentiful; soldiers came home after the war trained in working with heavy machinery. They took over the family farms and modernized with tractors, combines, and trucks. By 1950, draft horses were a rarity in the United States, and by 1954 there were only eighty-five Percherons.

It was the diligence of a few breeders that preserved the elegant Percheron and kept the breed going. A market still existed among Amish farmers, and as people gained more disposable income, the Percheron became popular in shows and exhibitions, and for specialized work like logging and small hobby farms. By 1988, the original 85 Percherons had increased to 1,088 and in 1998 to 2,257. Today the Percheron is America's most popular and prevalent draft horse, with 300,000 horses registered since 1975 and 3,500 members in The Percheron Horse Association of America.

Three-Percheron-team, Prince, Bud, and Bella, owned by Frankie Faithful, Nashville, NC.

**The distinguished type of the Shire is depicted in the art
of the Middle Ages.**

Shire

The Shire is believed to be the closest relative of the Great Horse of
the Middle Ages and was first bred as a warhorse in the 15th and 16th
centuries. Their distinguished type is depicted in the art of that time.
For this reason it is believed that the Shire is the oldest of the draft
horse breeds. The origin of the breed was the midlands of England.

It wasn't until the 18th century that the Shire became primarily
a workhorse. A breeder named Robert Bakewell is credited with im-
proving the breed and is referred to as the true founder of the Shire

as a breed. He imported large Dutch mares, mainly Friesians, and bred them to English stallions. He only bred those offspring that met his ideal for a high quality horse.

The Shire gets its name from its place of origin, the fertile lowlands of eastern England, in particular Lincolnshire, Warwickshire, Northhamptonshire, Leicestershire, and Cambridgeshire. First called the English Cart Horse Society, The Shire Horse Society of England was organized in 1878. Shire draft horses made their way to North America via London and Ontario, Canada, in 1836 to be used as artillery horses. A gray stallion named Columbus was imported to Massachusetts a few years later. In 1885 the American Shire Breeders Association was formed, and within a couple of years over 400 Shires were imported to America to meet farming needs. They were not as popular in America as other breeds because the farmers considered them sluggish and too straight in the shoulder and pastern, giving them a shorter stride, and they did not favor the Shires' long feathers, which attracted mud and dirt.

The Shire, considered the tallest and heaviest of all horses, is very powerful, able to pull up to five times their weight. Old records show that in 1924 a team in England was able to pull over 19 tons. That same year a single Shire pulled 29 tons, and another team set the new record at 50 tons. Foaled in 1846 in Bedfordshire, England, a Shire named Sampson, later renamed Mammoth, is recorded to have been the world's largest horse. He measured 21.25 hands (over 7 feet tall) and weighed, at his heaviest, 3,300 pounds. The Shire's average height is 16 to 17.5 hands high, but some reach 19 hands and weigh up to 2,000-plus pounds.

Most Shires are bay, brown, or black with white markings. Grays, chestnuts, and roans are acceptable. The head is attractive, with a broad forehead, and the profile is slightly convex, or roman-nosed. The neck is long and arched. The Shire has a sloping shoulder, deep heart girth, and strong, round hindquarters. The legs are longer than the Belgian and accented with long, silky feathering.

Like most draft breeds, the Shire's disposition is docile, with a willingness to work.

Once the Shire joined the workforce, one of its principle jobs was to deliver wagonloads of ale from the breweries to taverns. Shires still hold down that job at some of the smaller breweries because it is more economical to use real horsepower.

Given their great strength, Shires are often seen in pulling competitions. They are at home in the show ring as well and excel on the farm as a work horse, especially to pull heavy loads like hay wagons.

Shire Stallion, Dryt, owned by Roxanne Thrower, Camden, SC.

Suffolk Punch

The Suffolk Punch may well be the oldest of draft horse breeds. English farmers living in the counties of Norfolk and Suffolk developed the breed strictly for farming, probably as early as the 9th century. It is theorized that Vikings may have brought the Jutland Horse, a powerful and sturdy cold-blooded type, with them from

Denmark when they invaded England. Those horses are believed to have contributed to the breed. Because of the isolated geography of this English peninsula area, the Suffolk Punch has changed very little over the centuries.

The Suffolk Punch was an established breed with maintained stud records by the beginning of the 1700s. The foundation sire of the breed was called Thomas Crisp's Horse of Ullford, and he was foaled in 1768; all purebred Suffolk Punches alive today trace back to this one stallion.

Suffolk Punches were not as heavily imported to the United States as some other breeds. They were not as big as some of the more popular breeds, so were used to pull lighter loads and for farming. It was their longevity that caused them to become in demand in North America. This breed is known to stay productive well into its twenties.

Like other workhorses, they were abandoned in favor of gasoline powered vehicles and farm machines. Since the numbers were few to begin with, the Suffolk Punch almost went extinct in America during the 1950s. The Association was dormant from the 1950s until 1961, when they reorganized. Breeders began importing Suffolks again in the 1970s and 1980s.

On the critical list of the American Livestock Breeds Conservancy, the Suffolk Punch is making a slow comeback, and today there are about 800 to 1,200 horses in North America.

The head is attractive, with an intelligent expression. The Suffolk has a powerful, arching neck and is clean through the throatlatch. The shoulders tend to be straight for pulling power, rather than action. It has a strong back and well-sprung rib. The wide chest and deep heart girth give the horse great lung and heart capacity to account for his outstanding stamina. The hindquarters are long and smooth, and the horse carries a higher tail set and flatter croup that some breeds.

The Suffolk Punch stands on what appear to be short, strong legs. Part of that illusion is due to the stout body of the horse. The forearms and thighs are well muscled. The Suffolk does not have feathered legs like some other draft breeds. This keeps the legs from collecting mud in the fields. The foot is round, of good size to support the weight of the horse, and their hooves are known for wearing well, whether shod or not.

Breeders of the Suffolk Punch are fussy about its color—it must always be chestnut. No other color is allowed into the books. The shade can vary from light chestnut to a dark liver chestnut. Markings are minimal, with bold color not desired.

The soil of their home of origin is heavy clay, and the Suffolk Punch is very adept at working in those conditions. This ability to maneuver in sticky soil also makes the Suffolk an ideal logging horse. In recent years Suffolk horses have been imported to Pakistan for breeding as an army horse because of its tolerance of the climate.

Suffolk Punch Rudy owned by Jason Rutledge, Upperville, VA.
(Courtesy of Jason Rutledge of Virginia)

MINOR BREEDS

American Boulonnais

The Boulonnais of Northern France is believed to have descended from Roman horses brought to Europe when Caesar invaded Great Britain in 54 BC. Much later, during the Crusades and Spanish occupation, Oriental and Spanish horses were added to the mix. This background resulted in a draft horse with unusual elegance and speed. Like other draft breeds, the Boulonnais was first used as a warhorse.

Over time, two types of Boulonnais were developed to fit the particular needs of the people. A smaller Boulonnais, about 15 to 15.3 hands, was used primarily to pull fish carts from the coast to Paris. They were called *mareyeur*, which means "seller of fish." A larger type draft horse was developed mainly for farming beets in the 19th century.

Since 1991, every two years a re-enactment called the "route du poisson" is held to honor the Boulonnais mareyeur that used to pull the carts filled with fish from Boulogne to Paris. They made the trip back and forth as many as 25 times a day to deliver fresh fish to the markets.

Boulonnais draft horses numbered 600,000 in the early 1900s. Most of them were killed during the two world wars of the 20th century, and the mareyeur is nearly extinct today. The larger horses are managed and bred by government stud farms in France and number about 700 horses today.

In France the Boulonnais is currently used for meat production, and about 95 percent of all male horses are butchered. Only the best stallions are used for reproduction, even though the number of purebreds is low. The Boulonnais is also used for driving and riding, as well as farm and logging work.

The American Boulonnais Horse Association is promoting the breed in the United States. Breeders are importing purebred mares from France and artificially inseminating them with semen from stallions in France. Through these efforts American breeders hope to preserve this endangered breed.

American Cream Draft

A color breed and one of few drafts to claim its origin in the United States, the American Cream sprang from a horse in Iowa sold at auction in 1911. This cream-colored mare, known as Old Granny, was used in the breeding program of a man named Harry Lakin. She passed her color gene to her offspring.

The ideal American Cream Draft Horse stands about 15.1 to 16.3 hands and weighs about 1,600 pounds. The hair is cream or ivory white, with pink skin; horses may have white markings on the face and legs, and they have amber colored eyes, which set them apart from the American White Horse. Color should not supersede conformation and quality. The American Cream Draft Horse is well muscled, with an arched neck, and the head should have a straight profile. Living up to the gentle giant reputation of the draft horse, the American Cream has a willing disposition and is easy to train.

American Cream Draft Horses can be found on small farms in the Midwest doing what they were bred to do almost one hundred years ago: working. But they are also popular for carriage driving and pleasure riding.

Spotted Draft Horse

Spotted draft horses have probably been around as long as draft horses in general. In Europe, the best-known spotted drafts are the Drum Horses in the British royal stable, which are used in official parades. They are required to carry two large silver kettledrums and the rider. Strength and even temperament are important, especially since the rider's hands must be free of holding the reins so that he can play the drums. The reins are attached to the rider's feet.

In America, an Iowa breeder in the 1960s is noted for breeding for the color. The coloring of a team of Percheron-type horses named Dick and Jane that competed at pulling competitions is credited for creating a stir among the draft horse folk. Lowell and Gayle Clark owned the pair, and they eventually created two breed associations to promote and register pinto colored draft and draft crosses. The North American Spotted Draft Horse Association was formed in 1995 to promote and preserve the color breed. Spotted drafts can have any of the major draft breed foundations, although Percherons seem to dominate the registry. Gayle Clark started a second registry in 2002, the Pinto Draft Registry. Headquartered in New Mexico, this registry accepts pure spotted drafts and spotted half draft sport horses. Many colored drafts are registered in both associations.

American Spotted Draft Stallion, Sonny of Long Branch, owner, CB and Linda Daughtridge, Rocky Mount, NC.

**Old type Morgan, Reflectors Nemesis, owned by
Becky Beach, Wake Forest, NC.**
Photo by Becky Beach

Morgan

Although perhaps not a draft horse in the traditional sense, because
the Morgan is not a large horse, the founding father of the breed,
Justin Morgan (later called Figure) spent a good part of his life working in the woods skidding logs and in the fields plowing. His offspring,
all of which maintained a close resemblance to their father, were also
in high demand as working horses. The old type Morgan has a drafty
look, with a powerful front end well suited to harness work.

The Morgan is characterized by a refined head, a cresty neck and
powerful back, well-developed chest, and sloping shoulder. He is well
muscled, characterized by the long smooth muscle that gives him endurance. The average height is 14.2 to 15.2 hands. Today a more refined show-type Morgan has evolved, while the work type still exists.

The Morgan is now a popular pleasure, field hunter, and show horse, excelling under saddle and in harness. Though seldom used as workhorses today, they are excellent carriage horses, taking prizes in driving competitions all over the world.

Friesian

Not thought of as a draft horse today, the Friesian was influenced by the heavy horse of the Middle Ages. The Friesian dates back to the Middle Ages, originating in the Netherlands. It was used in farming and for transporting goods and people. In addition, it could carry heavy loads while under saddle. The Friesian nearly became extinct and no longer exists as the old type. A close relative, the Oldenburg, was crossed with the few remaining Friesians to salvage what remained of the breed. This resulted in a more refined horse than its predecessors. Today the Friesian is gaining in popularity in the United States both as a carriage and a riding horse.

Breed characteristics include a long mane and flowing tail, which often reaches the ground. The legs are heavily feathered, with the long leg hair starting further above the fetlocks than most draft breeds. The Friesian has a high head carriage and an animated trot, which gives it an elegant appearance. It is well muscled, but with a smoother muscle than on most drafts. Most Friesians stand 15 to 17 hands high.

The Friesian is well suited to a variety of jobs in the modern world. Its elegant movement and presence makes it a natural dressage horse. It is also showing up in carriage driving competitions. It is debatable whether today's Friesian can be considered a true draft horse since they are predominately used as pleasure and show horses and no longer have the bulk of the original type Friesian.

DRAFT PONIES

A pony is defined as any horse standing under 14.2 hands. By that definition any pony used for heavy work can be called a draft pony. Draft horses are sometimes crossed with pony breeds to produce a working-type pony. That combination can result in many draft-types that according to height are ponies.

There are even Miniature Horses that fall into the draft category. The miniature multi-horse hitch is a delight for spectators to watch in parades and exhibitions. It might be amusing to watch tiny horses pulling a tiny buckboard in a parade, but the fact is the miniature horse was first bred to work. Coal was an important commodity far back into history. At first the fuel was mined from the ground's surface, but as human demand increased men had to dig deeper, tunneling into the earth. They used small horses that could fit into the narrow tunnels to pull wagons of coal out of the tunnels. Soon horses were being bred down to size for the express purpose of working in the mines.

In the late 1800s, miniature—midget as they were called then—pit ponies were imported from Holland, Great Britain, and other European countries to the United States and Canada to replace women and children working in the mines. The soft coal mines of West Virginia, Virginia, and Kentucky had tunnels that were only 36 inches high, so the ponies had to be smaller than 34 inches.

Two draft breeds that are often pony-height are the Halflinger and Norwegian Fjord. Both these breeds have typical draft characteristics, except height and weight.

Halflinger

The Haflinger originated in the Tyrolean Mountains of Austria. In 1874 an Arabian stallion named Folie was crossed with the native mares. All pure Haflingers can trace their pedigree to Folie. These

Haflinger, Levi, owned by Debra Moorman of Wake Forest, NC.

hardy horses were used for plowing the steep mountainous fields, to clear land, and for packing in the rough mountain terrain. They were used for military packhorses during World War II. After the war, the Austrian government oversaw the breeding of Haflingers. Haflingers were first imported to America in 1958. Now there are about 10,000 in North America.

There are two types: draft and pleasure. No giant by any definition, the Haflinger stands between 13.2 and 15 hands. Smaller horses are not considered good breeding stock. If all other characteristics are outstanding, a Haflinger can go over 15 hands without penalty. The color is chestnut of varying shades, with a blonde mane and tail. Any deviation from this color is not favored. Facial markings are accepted, but not leg markings. The Haflinger has an elegant and harmonious build. Its head has an aristocratic look; a clean throatlatch ties the head into a medium to long neck. Haflingers are well muscled, with strong hindquarters. The draft-type Haflinger can still be found working on farms, pulling wagons, and skidding logs. The pleasure type is popular as a hunter, trail, and ranch horse.

Norwegian Fjord

As its name indicates, the Fjord originated in Norway. One of the oldest of breeds, it has been domesticated since 2000 BC. The Vikings used Fjords as warhorses and in the sport of horse fighting.

The breed is characterized by dun coloring with a dark dorsal stripe and leg bars. These markings, along with a black stripe down the center of the silver mane and tail, give them a primitive appearance

**Norwegian Fjords, Odden's Bjarne and Herger on a
beautiful winter's day in Wisconsin.**
Photo courtesy of Else Bigton.

similar to the Przewalski horse of Mongolia. The head is small and pony-like, and the neck is thick and muscular. They are strong and very dependable.

The Fjord is a good driving and saddle horse and well suited for farm work. They are very sure footed and can work in terrain that is difficult to work with tractors.

CHAPTER THREE

PREPARING FOR OWNERSHIP: HOUSING, TRANSPORTATION, AND EQUIPMENT

PROVIDING AN ADEQUATE FACILITY FOR KEEPING DRAFT horses takes careful planning before the purchase of the horse. While the general rules of horsekeeping apply to the draft horse, some adaptations are needed because of their size. Added dimensions must be considered in the amount of land required, size of the barn, fence height, storage room for feed and hay, and manure removal needs.

Step one in planning the draft horse facility is site selection. Several factors enter into the decision. The first thing to check is zoning, which can prohibit using the property for horses. Environmental regulations can also be a factor, as well as easements, deed restrictions, and covenants. Such regulations can be at state, county, or local levels.

Planning the layout of the facility includes the location of shelters and storage buildings, paddocks and pastures. Access, drainage, convenience to water and electricity sources, and room for expansion should be considered.

SHELTER

Depending on the climate, draft horses can usually do well outdoors as long as they have access to shade, protection from the wind, and plenty of clean water and food. The horse owner has more control in caring for and feeding the horse when they are housed in a barn. A barn also provides a safe environment for the horse and handler and saves labor and land costs.

While a simple run-in shed can provide the windbreak and shade needed, a barn with stalls allows the manager to separate horses from each other at feeding time, give them shelter in severe weather, and provides a place to isolate sick or injured horses.

Barn layouts typically fall into two main categories, each having a wide selection of designs. The simple shed row is more economical to build and works well for a small herd. The stalls are in a single row, with an overhang above the doors to keep out wind and rain. An aisle barn is usually two rows of stalls with an aisle down the center and one roof over all. The center aisle barn requires less land to house a larger herd. Variations include different roof styles and floor plans. Options include wash stalls, tack and feed rooms, and hay storage. When planning the barn, be sure to include space not only for the horses, but feed and hay storage, which will be related to the number of horses, and storage of tack and harness.

Two types of stalls are commonly used for draft horses: box or tie stalls. The box stall should be large enough for the horse to lie down and to allow the handler to work around the horse without being crowded. The minimum size of a draft horse's box stall is twelve-feet x twelve-feet; the ideal is fourteen-feet x fourteen-feet, depending on the size of the horse. Tie stalls take less space and are usually eight-feet long and five-feet wide. They work especially well for feeding and grooming horses that are turned out much of the time. Ceilings should be at least nine feet high. Stall doors should be at least four feet wide. If the draft horse is extremely large, a wider door might be needed. Doors larger than four feet wide should slide rather than open on hinges. The barn aisle should be wide enough for a truck or tractor to pull in for unloading feed and equipment.

Extra width and height may be needed for a draft's stall.

In planning the lighting in and around the barn, plan not only for your present needs but for future expansion, while considering costs, codes, environment, and barn design. National and state codes must be considered first. Electrical installations for stables and barns housing horses must be in compliance with NFPA 70 of the National Electrical Code, as well as local codes.

When dealing with horses, specific safety precautions have to be considered. Panel boxes must be in a dry and dust-free area; even when they are inside a building they must be made of weather resistant and non-corrosive material. Light fixtures must be installed out of reach of horses, keeping in mind the height of the draft horse, and fixtures must be caged to protect them from shattering if a horse rears or a worker gets a little wild with a pitchfork. Light fixtures should be placed so they are not in contact with any flammable materials, including hay and bedding.

Wiring must be run through approved conduit to prevent horses and rodents from chewing on the wires. There must be enough power coming to the barn to handle all electrical needs in addition to lights, such as fans, hot water heater, clippers, or radio.

If an existing barn was built without ground fault circuits, this should be corrected immediately. A portable GFCI power block can be used until the necessary upgrade is made. The power block, or "shock blocker," is plugged into an outlet, and then clippers, fans, lights, or other appliances plug into the blocker to prevent electrocution should a horse bite into the wires.

Most barns will require a combination of light sources, including natural, fluorescent, incandescent, mercury vapor, or halogen fixtures. Light from the sun, from windows or skylights, destroys bacteria and viruses, as well as parasite eggs and larvae.

OUTBUILDINGS

Because of combustibility and air quality concerns most horse advisors recommend a separate building for hay storage. One ton of hay requires about 200 cubic feet of storage. The hay barn should be large enough to hold a year's supply of hay.

Other structures might include an equipment shed, manure bin, shaving or bedding storage, and, if the drafts are to be ridden, a training or riding ring. If the draft horse will be used for driving or farm work, a shelter for horse-drawn vehicles and equipment will be necessary. Again, it is wise to leave room for expansion. Any equipment left outside should be kept out of paddocks or pastures and away from horses. Most horses have a talent for running into or otherwise hurting themselves on objects left in their environment.

FENCES

The primary purpose of a fence is to separate horses from where they should and should not be. The sheer size and height of the draft horse demand special attention to the design and materials used when making fences. In planning the horse facility, the placement of the paddocks and pastures depends on the amount of space available, location of the buildings, and access to roads, water, and shade.

In choosing fencing materials, the horse owner must consider safety, time, expense, and eye appeal. The best rule of thumb is to build the safest fence affordable, with esthetics factored into the budget. Using more expensive but more attractive materials where the fence is most visible, then using less expensive materials at the back of the property, is one strategy to stretch the budget and still enhance the looks of the property.

The strongest fence material is steel pipe. The pipe is welded on site, which makes installation expensive. It also must be painted every few years to prevent rust, but if this is done, the pipe fence will last a long time.

Wood, while being strong, is also expensive and requires regular painting and repair of rotted posts and boards. Polymer-coated wood is even more expensive, but saves on maintenance costs in the long run.

A board fence is attractive and sturdy. It should be 5 to 6 feet high.

There are a wide range of PVC fences on the market that are lower cost than the wood and coated wood, but are not as strong. There is also the danger of a horse being injured if it runs through the PVC fencing, which breaks with jagged edges.

An alternative to PCV is polyethylene rail. This fence encases multi-strands of high-tensile wire with flexible poly. It looks like a wooden rail fence. It can be run on wooden or metal T-posts. This type fence is low maintenance and relatively easy to install. The cost is in the mid-range compared to pipe, wood, or woven wire.

Woven wire is low cost and easy to install with either wooden posts or T-posts. It is most effective with a single wooden sight board at the top. These fences will last longer and do a better job of keeping the horses inside if they are re-enforced with electric wire or tape inside at the top and bottom. The hot wire will keep the horse from leaning on or reaching over the top, or sticking his head under the bottom to nibble that grass that is always greener on the other side. Another plus to the woven wire fence is that it will discourage dogs from entering the pasture.

**A wheel mounted on the bottom corner will hold the gate up
and make opening and closing it easier.**

Electric fencing by itself is the least expensive choice, but will prove useless if the power is interrupted, or if the horse becomes so spooked it ignores the shock and runs through it. Electric tape or braid has the advantage of high visibility, and it offers some give if a horse runs into it. The electric wire, tape, or braid should be attached to wood or metal T-posts spaced at no more than twelve-foot intervals to prevent sagging.

Barbed wire and high tensile wire are not good choices for horse fences. They can cause serious injury to horses that become entangled in them.

Fences for draft horses should be five to six feet high. Rails should be spaced about eight inches apart. Inspect the fence regularly to be sure it is free from projections such as wire or nails that can injure the horse.

Build gates wide enough to drive the tractor or truck through so the pastures can be mowed. It should have horse-proof latches. The gateposts should be heavier than the regular fence posts to support the weight of the gate. Wide gates will need extra support to prevent warping and sagging. A wheel mounted on the bottom corner will hold the gate up and make opening and closing easier, or the gate can be supported by a cable running from the opening end to a higher post at the hinged end to prevent sagging.

Some horses have been known to lift a gate off its hinges while grazing under the fence or while sticking its head through spaces in the gate. To prevent this, attach a hinge guard over the hinges, which can be a simple block of wood.

TRANSPORTATION

Most horse owners eventually need a way to transport their horses. The standard horse or stock trailer might not be suitable. Because of the draft horse's weight and size, the trailer must have adequate height and width dimensions, in addition to extra floor support,

heavy-duty tires, and a wider and stronger axle. Many draft horse owners find a slant load-style trailer does not provide the length needed for
large breeds, unless they remove one of the partitions. There are manufacturers that build extra wide trailers, with seven-foot, six-inch and
even eight-foot high models. Some manufacturers will also build cus-
tom designed trailers to comply with draft horse owners' needs.

Those who haul teams to events and shows often van the horses
and their horse-drawn vehicles in a tractor-trailer. Some are even
transported by rail.

Maintenance is the key to hauling horses safely. Before every trip
the following inspections should be made:

- Tires and spare tire: Check air, tread, and damage.
- Floor boards: Check for rot; replace as needed.
- Lights inside and outside trailer
- Brakes
- Welds, hinges, hitch
- Protruding screws, bolts, or anything that can injure the horse

At least annually check the following and make needed repairs:

- Framing and construction of trailer for rust and other damage
- Wiring and lights
- Lubrication
- Ramp and doors
- Wheels and tires

Rubber floor mats help prevent the horse from slipping and absorb sound. Bedding can also be added to make cleaning the trailer
easier. The bedding and mats should be removed after hauling and
the floor cleaned thoroughly to prevent rotting.

Certain state and federal regulations require a commercial license
if the towing vehicle, trailer, and load exceed 10,000 pounds. The
weight of one draft horse can equal that of two light horses, so it is important to check towing weight. This can be done at a grain elevator.

Horse trailers can be custom-made to handle the size and weight of draft horses.

There are restrictions in various states to do with height, weight, and length of the towing rig. Always heed the sign at weigh stations, because they are also used to check health papers, Coggins tests, registration, and driver's licenses. Not doing so can result in stiff penalties.

TACK, HARNESS, AND EQUIPMENT

Draft horses naturally require bigger equipment than light horses, and finding suppliers can sometimes be challenging. But as drafts become more and more popular, and with the help of the Internet, tack shops that specialize in draft tack are easier to find.

Once a supplier is found, careful measuring should be done before shopping for saddles, bridles, harness, training equipment, and horse clothing.

Blanket and sheet measurements are taken from the center of the chest, along the side of the horse, to the center of the tail. The inches in the measurement rounded to an even number will give you the blanket size. Most manufacturers make horse clothing up to size eighty-six. For larger sizes, horse owners may have to have them custom-made or altered.

A withers measurement will give the tree size for saddles. A special measuring tool can be purchased, or sometimes borrowed from a tack shop. Many shops allow customers to take a saddle on trial so it can be fitted.

English saddles with adjustable gullets and treeless saddles will usually fit drafts. Western saddles with Arabian trees will often fit a draft horse since they are designed for lower withers and rounder, flatter backs. Much of draft horse saddlery is hand-or custom-made, and that generally makes it more expensive. Used tack for draft horses can be found at auctions and consignment tack shops.

Draft horse harness traditionally is made of leather, and that is still the preferred material for show harness. Work harness is also made from nylon and plastic-coated nylon, which are easily cleaned with soap and water. Synthetic materials are lightweight and stay flexible in cold weather.

Care and proper storage of tack and harness will greatly extend its use and safety. Clean off sweat and grim after every use, and give it a thorough cleaning regularly. When doing a thorough cleaning, take the tack or harness completely apart. Inspect all the parts for worn or weak places. The first areas to wear out are the points where straps are buckled. Readjusting so the straps are buckled in a different hole periodically will extend the life of the tack.

After cleaning with saddle soap, condition leather with oil or another leather conditioning product. Do this before the leather is completely dry to moisturize it. Clean nylon equipment with soap and water after disassembling it and checking for wear and tear.

Store tack and harness in a clean, dry environment. Harness boxes are ideal for keeping dust and grime from accumulating. Options include a simple cupboard in which the harness is hung, or a nicely finished and portable box with a glass door that can travel from the tack room at home to shows.

Store tack in a clean and dry environment.

CHAPTER FOUR

BUYING YOUR FIRST DRAFT HORSE

WHEN BUYING A HORSE OF ANY TYPE, THE SINGLE MOST important consideration is what you want to do with the horse. This is definitely true of draft horses, since they vary in breed, type, and talent. You may be attracted to the draft horse because you attended a draft horse event and fell in love with them, or because you need the size and strength of the draft to pull a wagon. Perhaps you want to compete in pulling contests, or maybe you want to crossbreed a draft with a light horse to produce a sport horse. Whatever the purpose you have in mind, there will be a draft horse to fit your needs.

Age, breed, sex, training, color, conformation, size, and even location can all affect the market value of a horse. To get a general idea how much a draft horse that fits your needs will cost in your area, study breed journals and ads in newspapers and local publications. Attend a draft horse auction strictly to observe and take note of prices. The county livestock agent or horse specialist is a good resource person, since he or she will know of draft horse breeders and dealers in the area. All of this research will pay off in the long run to prevent buying on impulse and then suffering from buyer's regret.

A first-time draft horse owner should have someone who is not associated with the owner or the owner's agent help you evaluate the horse before you make a commitment. It is always advisable to have a veterinarian do a pre-purchase exam on a horse before the final deal is closed.

INDIVIDUAL SELLERS

Many first-time buyers find their horse by word-of-mouth. One of the most common resources for finding horses for sale is newspaper classifieds and magazine or online ads. Horse dealers are another source. These can be riskier ways to find a horse since you do not know the horse's history. Take an experienced horse person along to help evaluate the horse. Don't be pressured into a quick decision and stay within your price range. It is also important to check the horse's color and markings against those recorded on its Coggins test and registration papers if it is a registered horse.

When shopping for horses through ads, it is good to learn to read between the lines. If the ad says, "needs experienced owner" or "spirited," the horse more than likely is not a good candidate for a first-time buyer. It is wise to look at several horses before making a decision. It's fine to go back and look again before settling on which horse to buy. When you look at a horse, it is reasonable to ask to see it do what it is advertised to do: drive, plow, pull, or be ridden. If you have the skills already, you should also try out the horse.

BREEDERS

A breeder is an ideal place to find a young horse or breeding stock, but not for a first time buyer. While buying from a breeder gives the advantage of being able to see the parents and siblings of a horse, it is not usually a good opportunity to find trained horses. A buyer looking for stock to crossbreed with light horses can benefit from visiting the breeders for a proven broodmare or breeding stallion. There are usually a number of horses to choose from, and the breeder will be knowledgeable about the pedigrees and show records of the horses and their parents. Most of the breed associations have a list of breeders in each state. Draft horse magazines and Web sites also have breeding farm ads and lists.

A breeder is a good place to buy a young horse or breeding stock.

SHOWS

Draft horse shows are a good place to find horses for sale and to net-work among owners and breeders to find a draft horse. It is also a good place to observe horses in various classes, both in hand and in hitch, to decide what type draft horse you want to buy. Draft horses are shown in both open draft horse shows and breed shows.

ADOPTION AND RESCUE ORGANIZATIONS

Adopting a draft horse through a rescue agency can be an economically good move, but is not without some drawbacks. Usually adoption entails following the agency's rules on how the horse may be used and housed, and there can be limits to ownership and against transferring ownership. There will be an adoption fee, which goes toward covering the agency's expenses. Often the rescued horse has had veterinary care and rehabilitation before it is given up for adoption. The agency will send representatives to inspect the horse's new home and will probably re-inspect the facility periodically after the

Tara Harvey bought her Percheron, Shira, a PMU mare, from Hedgeville Stock Farm of Manitoba, Canada. Shira delivered a colt, HH King's Elohiym, a few months later.

horse is adopted. Still, if the new owner is willing to agree to the agency's stipulations and wants to give a home to a horse that needs one, adoption can be very rewarding.

Buying horses from PMU ranches is another way to acquire a draft horse for a small sum, sometimes for a few hundred dollars. The novice should proceed with caution. A young horse is not an ideal first horse, and some of these horses have health problems. But with the help of an experienced horse person and a veterinarian's clean bill of health, this may be an economical source for acquiring a draft horse.

A PMU ranch is one in which horses are kept for the production of pregnant mare urine (PMU). Pharmaceutical companies use urine from pregnant mares to extract the hormone estrogen. From this comes the product Premarin®, which is used for hormone replacement therapy in women. Draft horses, because they are larger, produce more urine than light horses. For that reason the industry favors using draft horses. The industry produces thousands of young draft horses, since the mares must be pregnant to produce the urine from which estrogen is extracted.

AUCTIONS

The advantage of draft horse auctions is that they offer a large number of horses to choose from. Major draft horse auctions offer hundreds of horses, as well as equipment and horse-drawn machinery and vehicles, for sale. They are also good places to network and meet draft horse owners. Before auction day, prospective buyers can order a sale catalog that has information about the horses being offered for auction.

Major draft horse auctions have a sale committee that inspects the horses and rates them according to their ability to hitch and drive. Defects found by the committee are required by law to be announced.

The sellers are also required to disclose any defects they know about in the horses they are running through the auction.

Even with all of these precautions, the novice should take an experienced horseman with expertise in draft horses and auctions to help make a wise choice. Even with careful observation, the help of an expert, and the legal regulations, an auction is a risky way to buy a first horse. Buyers do not normally have the opportunity for a pre-purchase vet exam when buying at an auction.

INSPECTING A PROSPECTIVE HORSE

When looking at a prospective new draft horse, some general observations can rule out some horses before going to the expense of a pre-purchase vet exam. First, stand back and look at the whole horse. Look for a picture of harmony and balance. Does the front end match the rear end? Is the back swayed or roached? Either defect defines weakness. Is the coat shiny and healthy looking? Does the horse have a good weight? Too much fat can cover up some conformation defects and may indicate poor health. A thin horse could have a heavy internal parasite infestation or other problems.

Next, take a closer look. Are the feet healthy or cracked and chipped? Pick up the feet and examine the sole for bruises, thrush, or hoof wall separation. Look for swelling of the leg joints. Feel for puffiness, heat, and hard or soft bumps on the legs. In addition, listen to the horse breathe. Does it sound normal?

Watch the horse move and look for signs of lameness: limping, head bobbing, pinned ears indicating discomfort. Listen to it breathe again after exercise. Loud or labored breathing can indicate lack of conditioning or more serious problems.

While some of these issues may only indicate minor, temporary problems, they at least warrant a closer look by a veterinarian before buying.

CHAPTER FIVE

HEALTH AND CARE OF THE DRAFT HORSE

KEEPING THE DRAFT HORSE IN GOOD HEALTH BEGINS WITH proper nutrition and continues with regular preventive measures, including vaccinating against disease, deworming, knowledge of common health problems and their symptoms, and careful observation. Knowing the symptoms of the most common horse ailments, learning to check the horse's vital signs, and examining the horse daily so that any problems are caught in the earliest stages will contribute to the horse's good health.

NUTRITION

Pasture grass is the most natural food for all horses, and draft horses are no exception. Forages, which include grass and hay, should make up the largest part of their diet. Since many draft horses are working horses, depending on their work load, they might need concentrates to supplement the forages. Horses are fed according to their weight, and since many draft horses weigh twice as much as most light horses, their daily ration will be considerably more. Your county extension office can provide tables to help estimate how much to feed your horse. The kind of forage available will also depend on which region the horse lives. The county extension service can test hay to learn its nutritional content. All horses need water, energy, proteins, vitamins, and minerals to be healthy. Required percentages of these nutrients depend on age, size, and amount of work the horse is doing.

WATER

Water is the most important nutrient and is consumed in the largest quantity. Proper growth and the working of all bodily functions are

Quality hay can provide a draft horse with most of its food requirements.

dependent on water. A horse can only live two to five days without this important nutrient.

It is necessary that draft horses have clean, fresh water available at all times. Ideally, water should be about 55 degrees Fahrenheit to be most palatable to horses. Horses tend to drink less when the water is freezing cold. Water heaters made for livestock tanks are fairly inexpensive and should be used in cold climates to keep water ice-free. Otherwise, in freezing temperatures it will be necessary to break through the ice and refill the trough or water buckets, sometimes several times a day. Salt offered free choice will also encourage the horse to drink during the cool seasons.

In warmer weather, provide cool water. Be aware that exposure to sun and heat encourages algae growth, which in some cases can be toxic. Place the water trough in the shade and change the water and clean the trough often.

The rule of thumb is a horse will drink about one half-gallon of water per hundred pounds of body weight in cool weather, which increases to one and one-half gallons in hot weather, or when the horse is heated from hard work. Using that guideline, expect that a 2,000-pound draft horse will need up to thirty gallons of water a day in hot, humid weather. A horse should not be allowed to drink its fill of water when it has just been worked hard. Allow about one hour for the horse to cool down, walking in the shade. The horse should be allowed to drink two or three swallows of water every five minutes during the cool-down process.

ENERGY

Carbohydrates and fats provide energy for the horse. All carbohydrates yield the same amount of energy. One pound of corn yields the same as one pound of oats. It is important to measure by weight rather than volume for this reason. Fats generate two and a quarter times more energy than carbohydrates. Both forms of concentrated food are found in grains. Draft horses are prone to problems with carbohydrates and therefore may do better receiving energy from fats.

Research done by Dr. Beth A. Valentine, DVM, finds a condition called Equine Polysaccharide Storage Myopathy (EPSM) exists in approximately two-thirds of all draft horses. This disease causes massive muscle damage, and because it can reach advanced stages before the horse owner realizes something is wrong, it can be fatal. Research at Cornell University has found horses with EPSM are not able to get enough muscle energy from carbohydrates. Changing to a diet consisting of 20 to 25 percent total daily calories of fat derived from plant origins, and less than 15 percent total daily calories of starches and sugars has been very successful when the disease is caught early enough. In fact, Dr. Valentine writes in her article, "EPSM—Muscle Diseases in Draft Horses," "If you have a confirmed EPSM horse in the barn, it may be easiest to feed all your horses the same diet. Feeding a 'normal' horse the diet is not harmful." Research backs up her statement and shows the diet may in fact be better for all horses. EPSM horses put on this diet, along with exercise, early in the disease, are able to go back to work and perform with little or no muscle damage.

PROTEIN

Proteins are necessary to build tissue, repair worn-out tissue, and aid in body functions. Protein is circulated through the bloodstream to the cells. If the cell doesn't need the protein for repairs, it uses it for energy; if it doesn't need it for energy, it becomes fat. But it is not stored in the body as protein, so it must be in the diet daily to benefit the horse.

Quality protein is most important in young horses that need it for bone and muscle growth. A one-month- to one-year-old needs 16 percent to 18 percent protein, a one- to two-year-old needs 14 percent, and a two- to three-year-old needs 12 percent. After its third year, a horse will do fine with as little as 5 percent protein in its diet.

While it is true that excess protein will be stored as fat, it is not the most efficient way to provide the horse with energy.

VITAMINS AND MINERALS

Vitamins and minerals are needed for tissue growth and repair, to build red blood cells, and to regulate the body's functions. Vitamins are divided into two categories: fat soluble A, D, E, and K. The second group is water soluble, and includes B-complex vitamins and vitamin C. Fat soluble vitamins are stored in the body's fat cells and liver, and the horse has a reserve of these vitamins. They can also build up to toxic levels if the diet has too much of these vitamins. Water-soluble vitamins must be replenished daily.

The horse's bones are made up of 36 percent calcium, 17 percent phosphorous, 0.89 percent magnesium, 10 percent fat, and 20 percent protein. Vitamins and minerals must be in the correct proportions in the food ration, especially in young horses. Phosphorous deficiency can cause weight loss and problems absorbing fat. Excessive phosphorous can cause hyperparathyroidism, commonly known as big head disease, and enlarged joints. Selenium is another example of how too much or too little of a mineral can be harmful. Selenium is needed for healthy cells, which are necessary for disease prevention, reproduction, and growth. Selenium is found in the soil and absorbed by plants. At least thirty-seven states have selenium-depleted soil. On the other hand, places with acidic soil can have a concentration of the mineral, which in turn means the plant growing in that soil will have toxic amounts of selenium. Horses eating plants with this high concentration can suffer from selenium poisoning. An imbalance of vitamins and minerals can also cause horses to develop pica, a disorder that causes them to eat inappropriate things such as wood or manure.

PREVENTIVE HEALTH CARE

The first defense against many equine diseases is to vaccinate. Consult with your veterinarian about what vaccinations your horse needs and how often a booster is required. The most common diseases the horse should be vaccinated for are equine encephalitis, also known as sleeping sickness (EEE, WEE, and VEE), West Nile virus, rabies, flu, tetanus, and strangles.

Equine infectious anemia (EIA) is an incurable disease in the horse transmitted by biting insects or other means of blood transference. Many horses can be carriers without showing any signs of being sick. Most states require that horses be tested regularly for EIA with a blood test called the Coggins Test. Owners must show proof that the horse tested negative within a prescribed time, usually one year, before moving the horse from one location to another. This is not without some controversy, since positive-tested horses are required to be permanently isolated from all other horses or else euthanized. Federal and state laws require the test.

A regular deworming program is necessary to protect the horse against internal parasites. Draft horse owners need to know their horse's body weight, since dewormers are given according to body weight. Most syringes of oral dewormers contain enough for treating up to a 1,200-pound horse. One syringe will not do the job for most draft horses. Dewormers can also be administered in the horse's feed or injected. Horse owners should ask their veterinarian's advice to determine the best program for their horse.

Good hygiene is also a deterrent to health problems in the horse. Keeping stalls and paddock areas clean not only helps keep the horse clean, but also will discourage the presence of disease-bearing vermin such as rats and flies.

HEALTH PROBLEMS COMMON TO THE DRAFT HORSE

Azoturia, also known as Monday morning disease, is a metabolic disorder common in draft horses. It usually occurs after the horse has had time off and then is put back to work. Shortly after beginning work, the horse exhibits symptoms of heavy sweating, nervous behavior, rapid pulse, and muscle stiffness, especially in the hindquarters. The horse will be in severe pain and will experience muscle spasms. The horse's urine is very dark in color because of the red pigment from the muscle cells that are released into the bloodstream as the muscle fibers break down. If the horse continues to work, the symptoms worsen and the horse will collapse. In the most severe cases the horse can die from kidney failure, because the kidneys cannot filter the enzymes being released into the blood stream from the muscles.

The cause of azoturia may be linked to Equine Polysaccharide Storage Myopathy (EPSM), the condition discussed in the section on nutrition.

In her article "EPSM—Muscle Diseases in Draft Horses," Dr. Valentine writes, "We don't yet understand what puts them over the edge into massive muscle injury, but studies of muscle from horses with signs of Monday morning disease show that EPSM is a common underlying condition, and we believe EPSM is the cause of the disease. Whether or not all horses with Monday morning disease also have EPSM remains to be absolutely proven, but so far evidence suggests they do."

Again, prevention is better than the cure. The EPMS low carbohydrate diet is the best preventive measure. In the past, various drugs, including steroids, muscle relaxers, and minerals, were used to treat the disease once the horse had an episode. The EPSM diet has shown to be very effective in preventing further episodes when started in early stages of the disease. Exercise is also important to the recovery of draft horses suffering azoturia. They should not be in a tie stall, but preferably be outside where they can move around.

Shivers, or shivering is a neuromuscular condition found most prevalently in draft horses and draft crosses. It is easy to diagnose due to the unique symptoms. The symptoms are sudden jerking or trembling of the hindquarters, in which the leg flexes toward the horse's belly and the tail lifts and trembles in a pumping motion while the horse is backing. The symptoms can also occur when the farrier is holding up a hind leg during shoeing.

The cause of shivering is unknown, but there is speculation that it is inherited, or can be a result of neural lesions left from infectious diseases like flu or strangles. Trauma may also be a cause. Some feel there is a connection with EPMS, but other researchers question that theory. Treatment is limited to massage, acupuncture, and exercise. Adequate vitamin E and the mineral selenium in the diet also seem to be important in controlling shivering episodes. Unfortunately shivering is usually a chronic disease that progressively gets worse if the horse continues to be worked.

Grease heel, or scratches, also called mud fever, is a type of dermatitis on the back of the pastern. It can be a problem with draft horses, especially those with a lot of feathering. It is most often found in the hind legs. It is believed that the long hair on the back of the pastern coupled with constant moisture and poor hygiene are the causes. Symptoms are inflammation and oozing fluid that becomes crusty and scabby. By the time it is noticed it has usually been there a long time. To treat grease heel, first clip the long hair, then wash with warm water and mild soap to remove the scabs. A good home remedy is to cover the affected area with zinc oxide (baby diaper ointment). Keep the horse in a dry and clean environment. In advanced cases the vet will usually prescribe an antibiotic-corticosteroid ointment or even give the horse antibiotic injections.

Colic is not a disease, but a symptom that can have many causes. It is the leading killer of horses. Colic is a stomachache caused by gas, fluid, or an obstruction of the intestines or stomach. The horse shows its discomfort in several ways. Pawing, rolling, sweating, biting at its sides, rapid breathing, and lying down and stretching out are all signs of colic. The vet should be called immediately if these signs are observed.

Treatment depends on the cause, which can range from gas to a twisted intestine. The veterinarian may administer a drug to stimulate the gut or drench with mineral oil. Severe cases such as an obstruction or twisted intestine may require surgery.

Regular deworming, feeding quality hay and concentrates, a regular feeding schedule, plenty of clean, fresh water, and exercise can help prevent many cases of colic.

Junctional Epidermolysis Bullosa (JEB) is an incurable disease that is caused by a mutated gene found in 30 to 35 percent of Belgian Draft horses. In this condition the horse lacks the skin protein Laminin-5. The fatal disease causes foals to die within a week after they are born. Layers of skin are unable to stick to each other, and patches of hair and skin begin to rub off at pressure points, spreading to bigger and bigger patches. The hooves will also slough off and ulcers form in the mouth and on the tongue. It is a miserable and painful process. As soon as it is known to have JEB, a foal should be euthanized.

The good news is that in 2002 the gene site of the mutation was located and a DNA test can be given breeding stock to determine if they are carriers of the gene. Breeders can use the test to avoid breeding a mare and stallion that both are carriers.

HOOF CARE

A sound horse starts from the bottom up. Nutrition, genetics, the work the horse is doing, and its environment will determine the health of the hoof.

A balanced diet is the first line of defense in maintaining healthy hooves. If the horse is being fed a balanced ration and still has a hoof

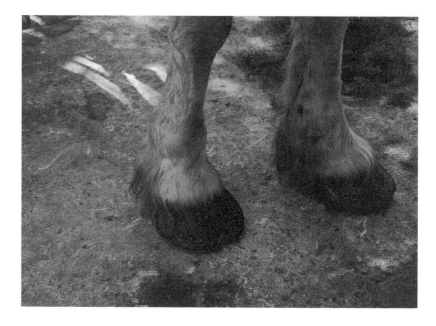

Draft horses are known for their "dinner plate" size feet.

that easily chips and cracks or does not hold a shoe on well, then supplements containing the B-vitamin Biotin, along with the essential amino acid methionine and the minerals zinc, copper, and manganese, may help promote growth and strengthen the hoof.

Supplementing should never be used as a substitution for good nutrition. It is also important to follow dosage instructions carefully since too much is not better, but can in fact be toxic to the horse.

Cleaning the hooves regularly is important to proper hoof care for the draft horse. Ideally, the hooves should be picked daily to prevent stone bruises and thrush. Anaerobic bacteria that originate in the stomach of the horse cause thrush. The bacteria are passed out through fecal matter, then are trapped in the crevices of the foot when the horse steps in it. The bacteria eat away at the soft tissue of the frog. Thrush is easiest detected by its foul odor and black discharge.

Picking out the hoof cleans away the fecal matter and exposes the hoof to the air, which prevents thrush. It is also helpful to keep the draft horse's stall and paddocks clean of manure. Treatment of thrush is easy if caught early. Apply an antiseptic agent until all signs are gone.

Cracked and chipped hooves are a common problem if the draft horse's environment is too dry. If the frog is dry, it loses its elasticity and ability to absorb shock when the hoof hits the ground. This can lead to lameness. An old time remedy, axle grease or burnt cylinder oil applied to the hoof, will actually seal out moisture and cause the hoof to be even drier. A better approach to try is to wet the ground around the water trough by letting water run over when filling it. The hoof will absorb some of that moisture while the horse stands to drink. Packing the hoof with wet clay will keep the bottom of the hoof moist. Moisturizing hoof ointments are available. Do not cover the whole hoof, but apply only to the live tissue at the cornet band.

Not all draft horses need to be shod. In fact, most of the time the hoof is better off without shoes. Still, there are times when shoes will protect the foot from bruising, cracking, and splitting. Shoes will also provide a pulling horse with better traction, and horses that work on pavement need shoes because the hoof wears down from the friction of working on such a surface. Show horses are shod for cosmetic reasons and sometimes to enhance the horse's action. Shod horses should have their shoes reset every six to eight weeks. Horses that are shod should have a break and go barefoot periodically. Without such breaks they will be more likely to develop contracted heels, weak hooves from the nail holes, and dry, brittle hooves. Many horse owners leave their horses barefoot in the winter while the horses are not being worked.

Shoeing stocks, once primarily used only by the Amish, are making their way into mainstream farriery. Farriers use shoeing stocks when working with difficult draft horses, or where there are several horses to be shod or trimmed. This keeps the heavy horses from leaning on the farrier while he or she works and restrains the unruly ones. The horse is restrained within the stocks, and the hoof to be worked on is strapped to a small platform built onto the stocks. The farrier's hands are then free to work, and the stocks save his or her back from excessive strain.

Steve Wisnieski, professional farrier from Sealy, Texas, has a lot of experience shoeing and trimming draft horses. He says stocks are just the best way to handle working with the big horses because, first of all, they often are not trained to stand and pick up their feet for the farrier.

Wisnieski said, "Keep in mind, I am under a horse almost every day of the year, so I see a lot more variety than most owners do. Stocks aren't always just for misbehaving horses either. There are quite a few EPSM horses out there that are unable to stand for the farrier. Stocks are a godsend for them as well as the farrier. Also you have injured horses that do so much better in stocks."

DENTAL CARE

A study done by Australia's Rural Industries Research and Development Corporation shows that when compared to light horses, some draft horse's teeth wear faster, perhaps because they eat more and spend more time chewing. The *Canadian Veterinary Journal* reports that a study of 298 non-racing horses on Prince Edward Island showed 30 percent of the draft horses had molar hooks, three times that of the light horses and miniature horses in the group.

Dental hooks are sharp edges on the teeth caused by uneven wear. These hooks can be very painful and cause the horse to have trouble eating. Slobbering, dropping food, and not eating are signs a horse might have dental hooks. Having the vet float (file) the horse's teeth usually will remedy the problem.

Kim Mack's Clydesdale, Ideal, in the shoeing stocks.
Photo courtesy of Rebecca Rudat

Wolf teeth, which are small teeth in front of the premolars, often cause irritation to the horse when the bit comes in contact with them. Dental bumps occur when the wolf teeth do not fully erupt. This can also be painful. Signs that wolf teeth are causing a horse pain are head tossing or carrying the head to one side when in the bridle. The vet can remove these teeth to relieve the pain.

It is advisable to have the horse's teeth checked by a veterinarian or equine dentist at least once a year.

CHAPTER SIX

SHOWING THE DRAFT HORSE

THE MAJOR DRAFT BREEDS ARE SHOWN IN TWO MAIN divisions, in-hand and hitch. Some draft horse shows offer under-saddle classes, including lead line, trail classes, jumping, and dressage.

In addition to breed shows, draft and draft crosses are shown in open draft shows, non-breed shows, and carriage driving competitions. In any of these competitions, one should study and follow the rules of the organization regulating the show.

In draft breed shows there are some differences in technique according to the breeds. In general, Percherons and Belgians follow similar rules, and Shires and Clydesdales have similarities. To avoid confusion novice showmen and women should observe a show and ask questions before attempting to show their own horses.

In-hand classes are judged on the horse's conformation, soundness, the way the horse moves, and quality, which—especially in mare and stallion classes—include breed character. In-hand classes are divided by the sex of the horse (mares, stallions, and geldings) and into age groups (foal, one-year-old up to under age three, and three and over.)

Craig H. Wood and Stephen G. Jackson write in their publication *Horse Judging Manual* (University of Kentucky Cooperative Extension) that, "All draft-type horses are characterized by their massiveness. Power, rather than speed, is desirable. In order to possess this power, the draft horse should be block or compact, low set or short-legged, and sufficiently heavy to enable him to pull. The head should be shapely and clean-cut. The chest should be especially deep and of ample width. The top line should include a short, strong back and loin, with a long, nicely turned, and well-muscled croup and a well-set tail. Muscling should be heavy throughout, especially in the forearm and gaskin. The shoulder should be sloping. The legs should be straight, true, and squarely set, and the bone should be strong, flat, and show plenty of quality."

All horses shown should be sound. An unsound horse is one suffering from any condition that hampers its ability to work. Lameness, blindness, and respiratory diseases are examples of unsoundness.

The movement of a horse is judged by its balance, hock and knee action, and stride. The horse should be able to move with efficiency so as not to waste energy and thus tire easily. The draft horse should move straight with a long, ground-covering stride. The conformation of the horse will directly influence its way of going. A sloping shoulder and pastern will result in a better moving horse than one whose angles at the shoulder and pastern are straight.

Quality is a little harder to define. It is the overall look of the horse, the total picture of conformation, muscling, bone, coat, and breed character. Conformation refers to how a horse is built and is directly related to its ability to perform. A draft horse should be well muscled for optimum strength. The muscles should be long and smooth for better endurance. The judge will look for flat cannon bones for better tendon attachment; again this results in more strength and endurance for a working horse.

A lustrous coat helps give the impression of a quality horse. While grooming is important in achieving a shiny coat, good nutrition is the real key to a healthy bloom that no brand of shampoo or conditioner can give the horse's coat.

Breed character is what makes a horse look like its breed. It is more important in mare and stallion classes than gelding classes, since breed character can be passed from generation to generation. The judge should imagine which horse most obviously and best represents its breed. Breed character most often starts with the head, then the top line. Other characteristics like feathering and color also help distinguish a breed.

In group classes, get of sire (one sire and two or three of his offspring) and produce of dam (one mare and two of her offspring), the judge, after considering the already mentioned points, must decide which horses possess the most reproductive likeness and uniformity of quality when comparing the offspring to the parent horse.

GROOMING FOR SHOW

A well-groomed horse tells the judge you take the show seriously and want to present your horse looking its best. It also shows respect for the show. A great deal of time and money goes into producing a show, and it is what it is: a show. The public is watching, and so are your peers, friends, and family. They are there to cheer on their favorite horses. While a horse show is a competition, it is also a public appearance. Appearing in scruffy attire and presenting a dirty horse is just plain bad manners.

The first job is a bath. This is usually done at home a day or so before the show. There are numerous products designed for bathing horses, enhancing their color, and conditioning manes and tails. Gray and pinto horses present the biggest challenge since light hair shows dirt and stains more easily, and the tails may be yellowed from urine. Special shampoos have whitening agents to remove the yellow. A home remedy is a bleach water rinse. After bathing the tail, rinse with a solution of five gallons of water with ¼ cup laundry bleach added. Dip the tail in the mixture. Wait fifteen minutes, then rinse in clear water. Add a conditioner according to the product's directions.

Grooming for the show begins with a bath.

If the show is a multi-day event, and if the horses get sweaty and dusty, it will be necessary to rinse the horse after it finishes its class, but probably a full bath isn't necessary unless the horse has rolled or the grounds are muddy.

CLIPPING

Clipping gives the horse a neat appearance and accents the head, adding a certain amount of refinement to the overall picture of a well-groomed specimen. The Percherons' and Belgians' heads, ears, and bridle path are clipped. Also clip around the coronary band of the hoof. The bridle path should be about four fingers wide.

Clydesdales and Shires should only have their ears and bridle path clipped. Never clip the hair from their legs, since the long, silky feathering on their fetlocks is a breed characteristic.

Clip after the horse has been washed to save wear and tear on the clipper blades. Dirt and grit will dull the blades. Many horses are afraid of the noise clippers make and need to be acclimated to the sound and vibrations by holding the clippers against the horse and gradually moving them closer to the head and ears as he gets used to them. Clipping takes practice even on a willing horse, ideally before show season. Clip in one continued movement to avoid leaving gouges and blade tracks. When clipping the hair around the coronet band, bring the clipper blade from the hoof working up and under the hair, and move the blades away so not to gouge into the leg hair.

MANES AND TAILS

Manes and tails require special attention. The mane should be brushed to the right side of the neck. This is not something you can do the day of the show. Most manes do not naturally fall on one side, but usually hang on both sides of the neck. To train it to the right requires frequently brushing it to that side, then braiding the mane, holding it down tightly so it will lay flat. Unbraid, brush, and re-braid regularly.

Whether to braid for the show or leave the mane loose depends on the breed and sex of the horse. Percheron and Belgian mares' manes are kept loose and their tails knotted or braided. The Clydesdale and Shire mares' manes may be left loose or braided; the forelock is always braided and tucked back under the halter. The mare's tail is always braided or tied. All breeds of stallions and geldings go with braided manes and tails.

Some show grooms recommend not combing the mane and tail when getting ready for show season, but to use your fingers to separate the hairs, to minimize hair breakage.

Braiding the mane and tail requires practice before the show. The best way to learn is from an experienced show groom, but instructions

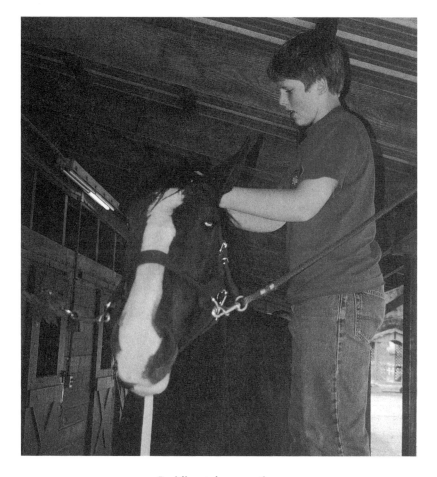

Braiding takes practice.

can be found in books, magazines, and on Web sites. A braiding bench or some sort of step stool is recommended so the work can be done while looking down at the horse's mane. The mane is braided in a tight French braid down the top of the neck with two contrasting colored strips of fabric braided in with the hair. This is called a rolled mane. Flowers or bows are tied along the crest. In halter classes there are seven flowers. In hitch use only five, to leave room for the harness.

The draft horse's tail is braided in a mud knot if the tail is docked. Docking tails is a controversial subject. A portion of the tail, either surgically or by banding, is removed. The procedure dates back to ancient times. Tradition says tails were docked on warhorses to prevent the enemy foot soldiers from grabbing the tail and clambering up on the horse to kill the rider. In modern times it was done to prevent the tail from becoming tangled in the lines when the horse was being used for plowing or driving. It has become a matter of style in some show horses.

In the surgical procedure the tail is shaved and prepped. The horse is sedated and a local anesthetic is used before the tail is amputated. A flap of skin is lifted and sewn over the remaining portion of tail so bone is not exposed. Since the spinal cord runs to the end of the tail, infection is a major concern.

Banding is usually done when the foal is very young. The tail is shaved and an elastic band is placed between the joints at the length desired. The band cuts off the blood circulation, and the end of the tail below the band eventually dries up and falls off.

The amount of hair that will grow from the docked tail varies. But even with long hair, it is more difficult for the horse to swat flies, and since the horse cannot hold the tail away from its body when it defecates, hygiene is a concern.

Docking is considered inhumane by some people and is illegal in the District of Columbia, California, Connecticut, Illinois, Maine, Massachusetts, Michigan, Minnesota, New Hampshire, New York, Ohio, and Washington. In New York it is also illegal to show a horse with a docked tail in most instances. Be sure to research your state's laws before you dock a horse's tail.

Undocked tails can be braided in a hunter-style French braid to the end of the tailbone, and then the remaining hair is done in a regular braid to the end. Clydesdales and Shires may be shown without braiding the tail at all.

HOOF CARE

Even the toes need special attention before the horse goes into the show arena. Percherons' and Belgians' hooves are painted with hoof black, including white hooves or white stripes on striped hooves. Clydesdales' and Shires' hooves are left natural. A little hoof conditioner will give their hooves a healthy look.

All breeds should be shod when shown. This enhances the size of the hoof and gives the horse a finished show look. A proper shoe job can also improve the horse's movement or way of going. A farrier who specializes in draft horses is a must. Some showmen like to use a scotch bottom shoe on their show horses. This shoe is beveled outward from top to bottom to give the illusion of a larger foot. Scotch bottoms are not appropriate when showing Shires. Sometimes clips, an extension of the shoe, are used to help keep the shoe in place.

APPOINTMENTS FOR IN-HAND CLASSES

Draft horses require little equipment for in-hand classes. Percherons and Belgians are shown in white leather show halters. Clydesdale mares are shown in white rope halters, while stallions and geldings of those breeds wear brown or black halters. Shire mares can be shown in brown or black leather halters. Generally, bays look nice in the brown or russet halter, while black is a nice accent for the black or gray horse. Be sure to use a matching lead line.

Stallions are sometimes shown using a show bridle and straight snaffle bit with a chain running through the snaffle rings and under the chin. In Scottish tradition, Clydesdale and Shire stallions wear a bellyband or stud belt. This resembles a surcingle, which goes around the girth area. A strap runs from the bit to the right side of the belt. This keeps the horse from turning into the handler.

The handler should dress cleanly and neatly. Proper attire is dress slacks and a shirt and tie or bolo. Ladies may wear skirts or slacks. Some barns match their shirts to the horses' braiding colors.

The handlers in certain breeds are allowed to carry a "show stick," which can be a fancy factory-made piece of equipment or homemade. The stick is about eighteen inches long and is used to prompt the horse to move over, set up, or lift its head. It is not supposed to be used to punish the horse in any way. In the United States, show attendants called trailers come behind the horse with a whip to encourage the horse to trot out with the handler. This should be done subtlety without extreme popping and waving of the whip.

Craig Miron, of Potomac Falls, Virginia, shows his Shires without a stick or trailers, which he feels can become a substitute for thorough training. He also chooses his in-hand horses carefully for presence as well as conformation. In choosing a horse to show in-hand, he says, "If your horse doesn't have the spark to show in-hand, don't show him or her in-hand. Maybe their talents are elsewhere. You can tell when they have that something to them, that presence that gets people going, 'Wow, look at him!'"

RING PROCEDURE FOR IN-HAND CLASSES

Routines may vary from breed to breed, or even show to show. It is important to know the rules and observe some events before entering a show. When leading the horse, hold the line in your right hand, and if carrying a show stick, hold it in the left hand.

The basic ring procedure is to enter the ring at a trot and line up where the ring steward indicates. Always lead from the left side of the horse. When turning, move out at a left angle, then turn the horse to your right, making a loop, or keyhole turn. This is a basic safety issue, because if you pull the horse toward you and turn around to the left you risk getting stepped on.

In the lineup, or whenever you stop the horse, turn so you are facing the horse while standing still and switch the lead to the left hand, the show stick to the right. The horse should be trained to stand quietly with its legs square.

When the judge gets to your horse he or she will usually ask you to walk the horse forward to the judge, then trot away. That is not set in stone, so listen carefully to any instructions the judge or ring steward may give. Some judges ask the exhibitors to walk in a circle around him or her and then to trot.

Practice at home having the horse travel in a straight line, moving forward willingly and standing patiently. Practice in different locations. A horse often works perfectly in a familiar place only to get antsy away from that safe space.

The trailer follows about ten feet behind the horse. Once the horses are lined up the trailer can come to the front, about ten feet from the horse, to assist in getting the horse's ears up. If the horse gets antsy the trailer can help keep the horse from turning around by moving to its side.

Youth showmanship is judged on the handler's ability to present the horse to its best advantage. The horse is basically a prop and not judged by its conformation or quality. The youth learn to groom, use correct appointments, and train their horses for in-hand classes. This is the ideal training ground for future showing as adults.

Some tips to remember: Keep your eye on the judge the whole time you are in the ring. At the same time keep your eyes up and look where you are going. Move the horse straight to the judge and then straight away, so the judge can see how your horse moves. When going away from the judge, glance back to be sure your horse is traveling straight. Don't be afraid to ask if you do not understand the judge's instructions. When coming to the judge, slow down before you get to him. Never crowd the judge or cause him or her to have to step back from your horse. Stop about ten feet from the judge or ring

Cleaning harness.

steward to pose your horse. Most important, stay calm and don't rush. Your judge will allow a reasonable amount of time to set the horse up.

In his book *It's Showtime!*, Robert A. Mischka writes that when a handler goes back into a champion class or group class, he should put the ribbons won in previous classes on the horse's halter or bridle. This helps the judge keep up with the horses he placed, especially in big shows.

Hitch Classes

Pulling is what draft horses do best. Hitch classes run from single- and two-horse-drawn carts to large team-drawn carriages and wagons. While the grooming of the horse is pretty much the same whether turning out a halter or driving horse, equipment and training are a great deal more involved.

The qualities that make a good halter horse should also be found in the performance horse, because conformation, soundness, way of going, and quality, along with proper training, will make it easier for the horse to perform well. The judge is looking for horses that move well, are sound, well mannered, and, in teams, horses that work well together. Show horses should move with nice knee and hock action, cadence, and deliberation. They should carry their heads up and have the look of a show horse. Any leg interferences such as paddling or winging will be penalized.

Most novices begin showing a single horse to a cart. Attending several shows as an observer, having an experienced mentor, and practicing at home all will help ensure a pleasant experience in the show ring. There are also driving schools that specialize in teaching how to drive draft horses. The novice should be well schooled in driving and have a well trained horse for the first time out.

The cart must fit the horse and the driver. A basic rule of thumb for fitting cart to horse is that the seat be level when the cart is hitched to the horse. The driver should have enough leg room to be comfortable, and his or her feet should reach the floor. This not only presents a pleasing picture to the judge, but is a matter of safety.

Just as important as fitting the cart to the horse is the fit of the harness. An ill-fitting harness can be dangerous and cause the horse pain and sores at contact points.

Again, out of respect for the show and pride in the horses, the harness and vehicles should be immaculately clean, with the harness cleaned and oiled and the metal parts polished.

To dress appropriately follow the same guidelines as in halter classes. When there are two drivers, as in multi-hitch classes, they should wear matching attire, usually representing the barn's colors. Drivers should keep their legs together for a neater look. Gentlemen should wear a suit or slacks with a blazer, tie, hat, and gloves at large shows. More causal attire is appropriate at smaller shows. Jeans are never appropriate at any show.

Ladies may wear slacks and blazers, pantsuits, or, in cart classes, dressier attire. Hats and gloves are also recommended. Junior exhibitors should follow the same guidelines. Attendants' attire should complement that of the drivers; usually with matching outfits in the barn's colors.

The driver should always have a whip in hand when driving a cart in the arena. When driving a team, it is permissible to put the whip in the seat behind you or someplace easy to reach. The entry number should be attached to the back of the vehicle.

Men's Cart.

Headers are allowed in driving classes. They stand at the horses' heads to steady them while waiting in the lineup. When showing a team, someone should ride sitting alongside the driver, in case of an emergency.

Junior drivers are required to have an adult in the vehicle with them when they are showing. It is advised, and some shows require, that junior exhibitors wear safety helmets.

RING PROCEDURE

The first rule of procedure is to be ready to go when you are called. Never cause the show to be held up waiting for you. Many shows eliminate entries that do not make their gate call.

Since it is never correct to pass another hitch, the driver must plan his entrance so he leaves his team plenty of room. Enter the ring at a trot unless instructed otherwise, going to the right of the entry gate. Driving deep into the corners can help with spacing.

Draft Tandem Hitch.

Farm Hitch.

Sometimes exhibitors will be asked to stop or walk while everyone arrives in the ring.

Judging is done at the walk and trot in both directions of the ring. When asked to reverse (meaning to change direction) cross the ring diagonally. It is important that drivers appear to be enjoying their work to give the best overall picture.

When the judge calls in the class, drivers should line up in the center side by side. Headers come in and stand at the horse's head, but should not touch the horse unless necessary. Horses should stand quietly. The judge will inspect each horse and ask the driver to back the horse. After backing, the driver moves the horse up again into the lineup.

Do not leave the arena until all the ribbons have been awarded. Those who receive a ribbon may then leave at a trot. The first place winner waits until all the exhibitors leave the arena to make a victory pass.

Clydesdale mares

Thundering hooves

Best friends

Spring plowing

Shire

Thanks, Mom

Snacking

Clydesdale foal stepping out

Team of three Percherons

Big, bold, and beautiful

Portrait of a lady

Tall girls

Pullin'

Standing proud

Mare grazes in peace at Quail Creek Farms

THE DRAFT HORSE PULL

THE PULLING CONTEST BETWEEN DRAFT HORSES, LIKE other contests of strength, stamina, or speed among horses, has its roots in pride of ownership. It probably traces back to the earliest times of domesticated horses. An impromptu challenge by one horseman to another and the contest was on. Maybe it was a couple of farmers with a wagonload of rocks, or two loggers seeing whose horse could pull the biggest load. One thing led to another, rules were made up, the contests were sanctioned, and the rest is history. Horse pulling was listed in an 1876 Tory, Pennsylvania, fair ad as entertainment. Horse racing was not allowed. Matches in the contest were held for teams, single horses, and mares.

All breeds of draft horses can be found competing, but Belgians seemed to dominate the field. In 1944 a team named Gene and Jake took the then-world record, pulling 4,175 pounds at a Michigan county fair.

Today's contests vary from region to region, but most fall into one of two categories: the contest using a dynamometer to measure horsepower and the contest using weights on a stone boat or sled. A horse pull is an elimination contest, with successful teams moving on to the next round, with weight added until there is a winner.

The dynamometer was invented in the 1920s by a team of researchers at Iowa University who were studying horsepower. They demonstrated the machine in a contest at the 1923 Iowa State Fair. The dynamometer works like this: the horse is hitched to the machine.

87

Weights are added to a sled as the horse pull progresses.

When the horse pulls against the collar, preset weights are lifted, which releases an oil valve; oil flows through the machine, and when the team stops pulling, the weights drop and close the valve. Each team is required to pull the preset weight 27.5 feet without stopping until all teams have a turn. The resistance weight is increased until only one team can pull the maximum weight set on the dynamometer. That team wins.

The stone boat or sled is loaded with weights, the team is hitched to the boat, and the horses are given either a time limit or distance in which to pull the load. In some contests the horses are given three tries to pull the sled the required distance, which is usually 27.5 feet. Here the rules vary again, with the distance being as short as five or six feet in small county fairs. Some contests require the distance be reached in one of three tries; others total the distance of all three goes, and if they reach the goal they are still qualified. When the horse stops pulling, the turn is over.

The contests are divided into two weight divisions. Lightweight teams weigh in at 3,300 to 3,200 pounds, heavyweights are 3,400 pounds and over. Horses are weighed on the grounds before the contest begins. Boundary lines are drawn on the ground and the finish line. Horses must stay within the corridor indicated or will be disqualified from the round. Hookers are assistants whose job it is to hook the horses to the sled or the dynamometer. Once they have done this, they are required to stand back and not speak to the horses or drivers. It is against the rules to slap the horses with the lines or strike them in any way. To be sure of the rules, it is necessary to contact the association governing the pull.

While there are no rules covering the grooming of the competing horses, most folks who compete want their horses to look their best. Pulling horses usually have roached manes, meaning the entire mane is shaved off. The ears and muzzle and the legs are also clipped to give a clean and neat appearance. The collar, harness, and bridle are made of much heavier grade materials than that used in regular

Draft Pull at Old Threshers Reunion, Denton Farm Park, Denton, NC.

hitches and most farming operations. There is a greater strain put on the equipment in pulling. In fact contestants are allowed to have spare equipment in case something breaks.

The pulling horse must be in top condition in order to compete successfully. Daily workouts and good nutrition are the main conditioning tools. Proper fitting of the horse's equipment is always a concern. Poor fitting harness will result in painful sores, and the horse will avoid the pain by not pulling. Harnesses need constant attention and readjustments since the horse's physique alters with conditioning and weight changes.

You might call horse pulling the NASCAR of the draft horse world. Stands are packed with spectators, and Web sites are set up highlighting favorite teamsters. Top dollar is paid for proven pulling teams, some into the five-figure range. Teams and drivers travel across the country competing. Pulling records are being set as this book is being written, as the giants of the horse world give it their all.

Terry Yoder and Chris Hatfield claimed the world heavyweight record in 2005. Hatfield drove the horses Mike and Buck to the win at the Hillsdale County Fair in Michigan, pulling 4,700 pounds 31 feet, 4 inches. Hatfield has competed since he was seven years old, when in 1977 he entered a pony-pulling contest. Both Hatfield's grandfathers competed, as did his father. He does about forty pulls a year all over the country, and between contests he works for Terry Yoder, training the horses.

In 2006, Hatfield and Yoder broke that record twice at the Pull of Champions in Syracuse, New York. Their team Roger and Oscar pulled 14 feet 2 inches on 5,000 pounds, and then they drove Mike and Smuck to 20 feet 5 inches on 5,000 pounds. But imagine the excitement in the stands when both those teams records were beaten at the same event by brothers Rick and Scott Brown of Acme, Pennsylvania, when their team Jim and Fred pulled over 5,000 pounds and set the new heavyweight record.

THE DRAFT PLEASURE HORSE

THE DRAFT HORSE IS NOT JUST AN ALL WORK AND NO PLAY equine. More and more horse enthusiasts are finding the mild temperament and size of the draft a good choice for pleasure riding and driving. Draft horses are showing up in local shows, gymkhanas, family outings, and of course on the trail. Breeder C.B. Daughtridge of Rocky Mount, North Carolina, says his best market for his American Spotted Draft Horses are pleasure horse owners, particularly the hunter jumper riders.

"Define pleasure horse," demanded one interviewee. And it is true; most owners of working draft horses will tell you they are a pleasure to own. To narrow it down, let's define the pleasure draft as one used for trail riding and driving and the occasional weekend show, or maybe one owned by the small breeder—essentially draft horses that are working companions. Still, it's hard to pin down what makes a pleasure horse a pleasure horse.

Hannah Johnson of Chapel Hill, North Carolina, found Quincy, her Percheron-maybe-Thoroughbred-cross gelding, on an Internet classified Web site. She fell in love with him the very first time she rode him.

Hannah had ridden a draft cross while in college and appreciated its temperament and attitude; plus she felt that the draft horse size complemented her height, a tall 5'10". She knew then she would look for a draft or draft cross when the time came for her to buy a horse.

Lisa Miller says her Belgian-Quarter Horse cross, Pete,
has changed her life forever.

While Hannah admits Quincy is not your typical event horse, she
has learned a lot from riding Quincy and working on that goal. She
says one of the biggest differences between light horses and drafts is
that it is harder to get the draft to engage its rear end. She surmises
this is due to the fact they have been bred to use their "front wheel
drive" to pull against a collar with their big chest and shoulders.

"It takes a huge amount of leg not so much to get him going, but to keep him going," she said. Still, she compares riding Quincy to riding a giant sofa, making him a comfortable ride on trails and when showing. Hence he has earned the nickname, "Quincy Couch."

Hannah also said, "I've found the feel of jumping with drafts to be different than on lighter horses. With that much mass to haul over a fence, you get a much better sense of exactly when the horse is going to take off than with a lighter horse."

Denise Pullis of New York breeds and trains miniature horses, so a draft horse wasn't really part of the plan. Denise first saw Liberty on the news. The Belgian mare had been seized by the local humane society along with several other neglected horses in an abusive situation.

Liberty had not been handled, had a mane entangled with burdocks, and her feet had not been trimmed in over a year. She and the other horses were so starved they had eaten the fencing, a tree, and part of the barn. Denise helped the rescuers work with Liberty for two years prior to reaching the final adoption. She visited and had Liberty broke to saddle during the wait.

Adding a draft horse to the miniature horse herd was pretty comical to see. Her hay dealer was fond of teasing his helpers by telling them they were going to a mini farm. Then when they arrived, Libby would stick her head out the barn door as if to say, "Surprise!" All 17.2 hands of Liberty settled right in with the little horses. Denise says she was very gentle with them. One in particular, a miniature stallion named Anakin, was quickly put in his place whenever he got out of line. Liberty would pin her ears and lift a hoof as if to say, "Do you want some of this?" which was as far as it went. Anakin would walk away and Liberty would immediately forgive his antics.

Just three years after coming to live with the Pullis family, Liberty was taken ill while Denise was in Mexico. At first the vet suspected colic, a twisted intestine. He recommended surgery at nearby Cornell University Veterinary Hospital. But the $10,000 surgery was out of the question for Denise. Over the phone she told the vet to put Liberty down.

Before Denise could get home the vet changed the diagnosis to anterior enteritis. He had given Liberty Banamine and pumped about six gallons of reflux from her stomach. Her condition was poor, but maybe, just maybe, she had a chance.

Denise expected to come home to a dead horse, but Libby was up and standing when she got to the barn. She was even greeted with a welcoming whinny from the Belgian mare.

"I was in shock," Denise said.

Liberty looked drawn, but she was nibbling her hay and drinking water. The vet thought if she continued to make progress she might pull through. That was Sunday.

On Monday Denise stayed home from work to nurse her sick horse. Sick herself with a respiratory infection, Denise went to the doctor. She came home and went out to check on Libby. This time Liberty did not whinny but came up to Denise and rested her chin on her friend's shoulder for a long while. Then she backed away from Denise, staggering. Denise checked her gums, which were dark red with pin-dots of blood. Denise recognized this as a sign of toxic shock. She ran to the house to call the vet.

By the time she got back Libby had collapsed into the electric fence. Denise turned off the charger but doubted the horse even felt the shock. Libby struggled to her feet, staggered, had a massive seizure, and died. The only guess by expert opinion was that Liberty's prior life of neglect had left her vulnerable to the condition that caused her death. Liberty is buried beneath an old pine tree on the farm where her spirit lives on in the good memories she left behind.

The void left by Liberty in Denise's heart led her to seek out another draft horse. She found a PMU foal rescued from an auction in Manitoba, Canada, through the Spring Hill Horse Rescue in Brandon, Vermont. Finisterre, French meaning "lands end," was her name. She was a Clydesdale cross, not even halter broke when Denise picked her up. The yearling had to be loaded into the trailer via chutes.

Denise let her settle in Liberty's old stall a few days before beginning her groundwork. A mini mare named Freedom took Finisterre under her charge. Denise said Freedom was the only mini mare without a foal that spring, so she adopted this big baby as her own. They are still best buddies.

Finisterre did well in her lessons. Denise started saddle breaking by getting on the mare's back one day while she was munching hay. Since then Denise has also trained her draft horse to do some tricks, including shaking hands, bowing, and answering yes or no on cue to Denise's questions. Denise looks forward to a long and pleasurable relationship with her big horse.

Terri Pierce is a horse trainer in Richlands, North Carolina, who wanted a bigger horse than the Quarter Horses and Arab she'd owned. What she ended up with were five draft horses: a purebred Percheron, a Percheron-Thoroughbred cross, a Belgian-Quarter Horse cross, purebred Belgian, and a Clydesdale-Quarter Horse cross. It's a good thing Terri is an experienced trainer, because all of these young (6 to 15 months old) horses came to her un-broke and semi-wild. Terri purchased the horses from PMU ranchers in Canada through a friend with connections to the industry.

"The personality differences are unbelievable," Terri said. "The earth could shake and she [the purebred Percheron] would look at you like, 'Wow, that was cool,' and go on eating." Terri has found her Belgians to be a little shier than the Percherons. She plans to take their training slowly, not riding until they are four years old. She also hopes to breed her Percheron when she is five to an Arabian stallion to produce a warmblood offspring.

No matter what they plan to do with their pleasure drafts, when folks talk about them, they use adjectives like sensible, safe, fearless, fantastic, goofy, a star, or love of my life, and they declare that now they are draft horse owners there is no turning back. "I wouldn't trade my draft for a whole barn full of fancy Thoroughbreds," declared one lady.

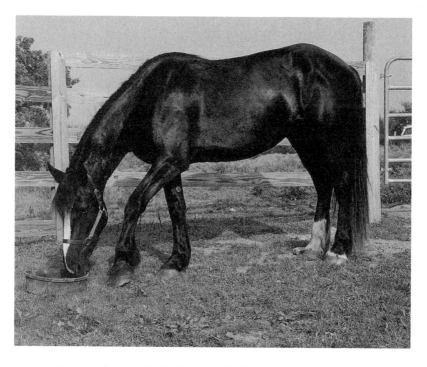

Amy Synder's PMU Percheron, Toby, loves attention and is a favorite with the whole family.

CHAPTER NINE

REAL WORK

MANY DRAFT HORSES IN AMERICA TODAY ARE EARNING their keep on the farm, in the forest, and in the city. Old traditions are kept alive and the skills required to farm and log or drive a team are being handed down from one generation to the next. The continued rise in gas prices and the fact that horses and horse-drawn equipment are much less expensive than gasoline-powered machines make it good economic sense in many cases to return to the old way of doing things. People who are using draft horses on the job say there is one thing that cannot be measured in dollars and cents, and that is their relationship with their horses.

CARRIAGE TOURS

One of the most popular methods of taking a historic tour is on a carriage drive. The charm of a good storyteller and a horse-drawn trolley or carriage adds up to good business in many historic communities throughout the country. Cisco, a Belgian gelding, and his driver and owner Rose, take tourists through the historic district of Beaufort, South Carolina. Cisco doesn't work all that hard, walking at a leisurely pace, stopping often at points of interest while Rose gives her passengers the details of the beautiful antebellum homes, colonial churches, cemeteries, and other historic sites. Even so, it's hot and humid in the Low Country of South Carolina, and Cisco gets a well-deserved ten-minute break in the shade after each forty-

**Rose and Cisco team up to give tourists carriage rides through
the historic district of Beaufort, SC.**

five minute trip. He is watered, offered a snack, and his diaper is
changed. (Sanitation rules require that horses wear a bag to catch
poops before they land in the streets.)

It takes a steady minded horse to take tourists through streets
where it is exposed to traffic, horns, sirens, fluttering trash, and a host

of other sights and sounds that would certainly spook the average horse. The draft horse's even temperament makes him a natural candidate for the job.

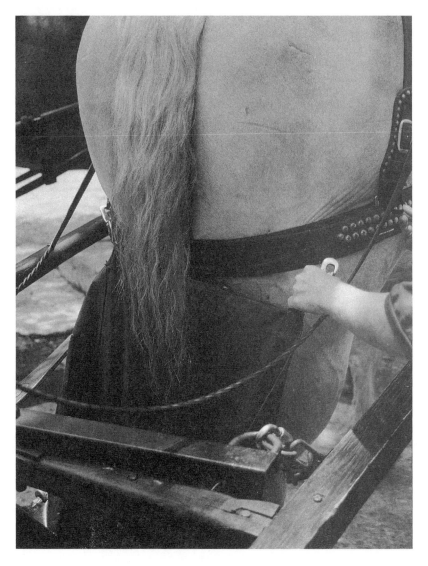

**Carriage Horses in historic Beaufort, SC, wear a "diaper"
so they don't litter the streets.**

Tourist Deborah Smith Brown thanks Cisco for a good ride.

FARM WORK

Farming with draft horses is still being done in this age of mechanization; the skills being handed down from one generation to another. Some farmers are using the draft horse for nostalgic reasons, but many are doing it for practical reasons. On small farms it is less expensive to farm with horses than tractors, horses do not pollute the air, horses are quiet, and perhaps the best reason to farm with horses is they do not require gasoline to run.

Fahlon Faithful learns the skill of plowing with her daddy's Percheron team.

Mr. Jimmy Dozier of Nashville, North Carolina, uses either of his two teams of Belgian and Spotted Drafts to plow thirty acres for corn. He also uses his horses to rake hay. He plans to use them for cutting the hay once he finishes restoring his horse-drawn hay mower. Basically the horses earn their keep this way, since most of the hay is used to feed them.

Mr. Dozier gets a little help from his friends by holding a plow day at his farm in the spring. Other draft horse owners are invited over with their teams, fed breakfast, and then the plowing begins. Friends and family gather and can get a plowing lesson, taking a turn cutting furrows in the warm Carolina earth. Teenagers attending the event are quick to give it a try and hopefully will pass their new skills down to their children one day. Soon the smell of barbequed chicken fills the air, the horses are given a break, and the crowd is treated to lunch. Then the plowing continues into late afternoon.

The plow day is an opportunity to share with the community how life was on the farm generations ago and to pass along the skills required to work a draft horse team to the generation to come.

Jimmy Dozier plows his thirty-acre cornfield with his Belgian team.

There are other farmers who do all or most of their farming with horses. Neil Dimmock, whose farm is near Edmonton, Canada, is a fifth generation farmer using real horsepower for about 80 percent of the work. Dimmock's family came from England to North America in the 1860s. His great-grandparents ranched and had two hundred horses. So the love of horses goes way back.

Dimmock's great grandfather started out with Clydesdales, but found they crossed poorly with the native stock. He sold them and went east and bought Percheron stallions in 1895. He trained and sold teams to other settlers, as well as using them on the family farm. The Dimmocks have had Percherons ever since. Neil Dimmock has six Percherons whose pedigrees go all the way back to the first ones his grandpa bought.

"I have and do drive anything, but my heart belongs to the big and black registered Percherons. The most intelligent and loyal horses that I have had the pleasure to work with have all been Percherons," Neil said.

Neil Dimmock holds the world record for driving the largest farm hitch and the largest Percheron hitch—forty-six horses. He hitched the horses to a twenty-six-foot-deep tillage cultivator built by Ezee-On Manufacturing that was designed for tractors with 130+ horsepower. The hitch measured 130 feet from Neil's hands to the lead horses. He made a special box that was eight feet tall so he could see over all of the horses. The Guinness Book of World Records would not add the agriculture category and only has the record for horses pulling a carriage.

The multi-horse hitch isn't just a stunt to break a record, though. Dimmock uses big teams to plow, seed, till, cultivate, and harvest crops every day. In addition to farming, Dimmock teaches others his skills. He also trains teams for other people and breeds and sells registered Percherons. He holds clinics at his farm, Hitch Masters Percherons.

Record-breaking forty-six horse farm hitch owned by Neil Dimmock.
photo by Kim Dimmock

When asked why he farms with horses, Neil Dimmock said, "Because I can, I like it, I know how, I have lots of horses, my kids can help, my wife lets me, I have one of North America's largest collection of working horse machinery, and, for me, it is economical."

Neil believes more farmers might turn to horses for their horsepower with the steady rise in fuel prices and that the future looks bright for the draft horse.

FORESTRY

Logging with draft horses is on the upswing, too. The logger can get into places with horses that are not possible with machines, and they can selectively cut trees while preserving others and preserving the land, especially in wetlands and other sensitive areas. Even setting aside the environmental pluses, it actually costs less to purchase and keep horses than to purchase, run, and maintain the heavy machinery used in the logging industry.

Jason Rutledge of Virginia is a special breed of logger. He is president and founder of Healing Harvest Forest Foundation and the recipient of a Rock the Earth Defender award for his work. Rock the Earth is a public interest group dedicated to preserving natural resources. They recognized Rutledge's work in forestry practices that aim to preserve the forests for the future generations.

Jason describes his purpose for Healing Harvest Forest Foundation as an organization established to develop, implement, and support community-based sustainable forestry initiatives through the widespread use of animal-powered (horse, mule, oxen, elephant) extraction of logs and "worst first" single tree selection of individual trees in timber harvesting

"Ours is a 'whole forest' eco-system management approach, toward the end of restorative forestry, community stability, and achievement of our mission statement."

That mission is, "To address human needs for forest products while creating a nurturing coexistence between the forest and the human community."

In his article "Modern Horse Logging," Rutledge writes that simply using horses to log does not guarantee a sensitive improvement or restoration harvest. He says it depends on the human operator.

He explains, "Our method of selecting individual trees on a 'worst first' basis and limiting removal to no more than 30 percent retains the forested condition and is indeed improvement forestry.

It is an example of humans behaving as beneficial predators. Not high grading or trophy hunting, but allowing the strongest to survive. The holes created in the forest canopy are substantial enough for 'shade intolerant' species to regenerate naturally from seedlings of the superior specimens that are left in a healthy 'good growing' condition."

Rutledge cites several advantages to using horses in logging operations. Their feet cause less damage to the forest floor and tree roots than heavy machinery. The horses are powered on solar fuel in the form of hay and grain, using less fossil fuel than machines. They also produce fertilizer rather than carbon monoxide, so they contribute less to global warming. Animals are self healing and renewable. They heal when they are injured, and Rutledge remarks, "No one has ever found a baby skidder in the woods one morning." He also points out the therapeutic benefits of working with a living creature.

As for economics Rutledge writes:

"Animal powered forestry is labor intensive and low volume production. This is often mentioned by conventional forestry interests as a negative feature of a heritage-based technology. We believe it is a benefit. Recent reports state that 40 percent of the forested land base in Virginia is in privately owned tracts of forty acres or less. It is finally being recognized that the current level of consumption of forest products is not sustainable with available resources and that these smaller pieces will have to be part of the resources base in order to meet human needs for forest products. This fragmentation of ownership and forest parcel size shrinkage is projected to continue under increased population pressure. Animal powered harvesting systems are low-cost enterprises that can economically harvest these smaller boundaries."

Advertising

The multi-horse hitch pulling big wagons loaded with supplies was a common scene in American history in the 19th and early 20th centuries. Cities bustled with horse-drawn wagons loaded with goods, moving them from ships and railways to warehouses and businesses, or carrying loads overland from city to city. Some of the wagons were works of art, as companies had them painted to promote their businesses. As the horses moved goods from one location to another they also carried moving advertisements for attracting customers along their routes.

Today you can still see these magnificent horses pulling beautiful wagons that are also moving billboards, but usually during parades or as an exhibition at festivals and horse shows. The famous Budweiser Team is just one of many hitches used to promote products today. They have been so successful that the Clydesdale is often referred to as the Budweiser Horse.

PHYSICAL AND MENTAL THERAPY

The draft horse can be valuable in various therapeutic programs. One innovative way horses are helping people is in equine assisted

Skidding logs, photo by Roey Yahai, www.rohai.com.

psychotherapy. The horse is used as a bridge between human emotions for the horse and relating those emotions to other humans. The Equine Assisted Growth and Learning Association (EAGALA) was organized to set a standard of excellence in the field where horses are used to improve the metal health of people participating in their programs.

Bruce Anderson, who uses Shires in his equine assisted psychotherapy programs, owns Natures View in Camden, South Carolina. He conducts a variety of programs including individual and group therapy with schools, corporations, and military and police training simulations. He says the Shire's size and disposition make them ideal horses for his program.

Roxanne Thrower owns the Shires that Bruce Anderson uses in his program. She says, "The reason Bruce Anderson likes to use my Shires, especially with police, is that they are big, most are black, and they present an unknown. Even though they are the size they are, they are so gentle."

Susan Taylor of Vermont conducts animal-assisted therapies and activities as director of the Newport Adolescent ~ Adult Programs with her husband's clinic, The Chrysalis Center for Human Development. Susan works with individuals, families, and groups and also uses draft horses in some of her programs.

Another program that uses draft horses for both physical and emotional therapy is the Circle of Hope Therapeutic Riding Center in Barnesville, Maryland. Some of their students are war veterans who have lost limbs while in Iraq and Afghanistan. The riding program strengthens joints and muscles and teaches balance, while also giving back self-confidence to the soldiers. While helping heal the body, the draft horse also helps the students emotionally as they interact with the horses.

Draft horses also fill the need for large, gentle horses in physical therapeutic riding programs. They make it possible for larger adults to participate in the programs.

EDUCATION

Draft horses are teachers in many capacities. You will find them demonstrating various old ways of farming, like threshing and logging, serving in military re-enactments, and even participating in jousting events at renaissance fairs to show how the draft horse was once an indispensable war machine.

Draft horses also excel as schooling mounts in many riding academies. Their size and substance allow heavier riders the opportunity to learn to ride. Their calm attitude makes them ideal mounts for the timid rider. Instructor Susan Bothern says the only real disadvantages to having draft horses in her lesson string are finding tack to fit them and farriers who don't mind working with the big horses.

Susan said, "Draft horses aren't slow or dull like the common perception." She in fact finds them playful and mischievous at times, and agile. She does find they have to work a little harder at using their hind ends, but that doesn't stop them from doing their job on the flat and over fences. Most important is the attitude and good work ethic of the draft horse. Speaking of one mare in particular Susan said, "She gave me 100 percent at all times."

POLICE HORSES

The draft horse has a long history of crowd control, going back to its day as a military mount in the Middle Ages. Today, their size and steady temperament make them ideal choices for mounted police units. The job of the police horse is mainly crowd control, but that's not its only job. The officers ride their assigned horses on patrols and in parades and ceremonies. The horses are good public relations ambassadors, with city residents enjoying meeting the horses as they patrol their neighborhoods. The big horses allow officers to get through crowds, such as sporting events and concerts, to give help when needed, and to make way for emergency vehicles. The police horse goes through a thorough training routine that exposes them to as much stimuli as possible, because they must be tolerant of all kinds of noises and sights.

Some draft horses have given their life in the line of duty and this raises public concern. One recent incident involved an eight-year-old partbred Belgian name Brigadier. He was a member of The Mounted Unit of Toronto Police for five years before an enraged motorist ran down the officer and Brigadier; then sped away from the scene. Brigadier's injuries were mortal and he was humanely shot dead by other police officers at the scene.

In response to Brigadier's death and the fact that the driver was only charged with destruction of property, a new law is being proposed in Canada. The law will make in unlawful to "knowingly or recklessly cause unnecessary pain, suffering or injury to an animal or cause pain or injury through criminally negligent conduct." This law will move animals out of the property code to cover animal cruelty with a fine of up to $10,000 versus the present $2,000 fine for destruction of property. The proposed law is called Brigadier's Law.

CHAPTER TEN

BREEDING DRAFT HORSES

BREEDING DRAFT HORSES IS NOT WITHOUT SOME STUMBLING blocks. The single trait selection for size in draft horses has resulted in some problems. Draft horses, both mares and stallions, tend to have lower fertility than light horse breeds, and pregnant mares have a high incident of dystocia, retained placentas, and twinning. In addition, newborn draft foals are sometimes weak and take longer to stand and nurse than light horse foals. The key to overcoming these obstacles is knowledge and preparation, plus the help of a veterinarian experienced in draft horse care.

The upside is that once a mare has successfully produced a healthy foal, she usually makes a very good mama that produces a large volume of milk and is very attentive to her foal.

Many months of preparation go into the production of a healthy foal. Selecting a quality dam and sire are the first steps. Indiscriminate breeding can only hurt the breed as a whole and is hard on the pocketbook of the breeder. Only the best affordable parent horses should be chosen as breeding prospects.

Before breeding a mare, a veterinarian should examine the mare and evaluate her ability to bring a foal to full term and check for any infections that can interfere with her fertility. Only after such infections are cleared should the mare be bred.

Infertility. Dr. Lisa Hale, DVM, writes in her article, "Reproduction Problems in the Draft Horse," that infertility in draft stallions is due, in part, to their slow maturity rate. As two-year-olds, their sperm

**Four-month-old Clydesdale, Katie, is the product of a
careful breeding program.**

count is less than that of light horse breeds. Dr. Hale states that the draft stallion's testicles are small in relation to their body size. These two factors result in poor sperm quality. This makes breeding by artificial insemination with a young stallion especially difficult.

Dystocia. Dystocia is any difficulty in giving birth to the foal. Dr. Hale also writes, "Although draft mares do not have a higher incidence of dystocia than the light mares, when they do have problems during foaling, the foal's large size complicates delivery further. For example, even if the foal is in the proper position, many mares need assistance to deliver due to inadequate uterine muscle tone and contractions given the size of the foal."

Draft and older mares are more predisposed to have prepubic tendon rupture, also because of their size. The signs of this condition are ventral edema, dropped abdomen, and bloody mammary secretions. Inducing labor or doing a C-section is usually necessary. Even then, the prognosis for the foal and mare is poor.

Retained placentas. Retaining the placenta is more common in draft horses than light horses. This is a highly dangerous situation to the mare's welfare and her ability to become pregnant again. If the placenta is not expelled within two hours of the foal's birth, the veterinarian should be called in. This is a narrower span of time than that recommended for light horses. The consequence of a retained placenta is uterine infection, which can cause the mare to become infertile, and if the infection becomes systemic, laminitis can occur.

Laminitis, which causes a crippling condition known as founder, is the inflammation of the laminae the connective tissue that bind the hoof wall to the foot. When they become severely inflamed, the hoof can actually slough away from the foot. It may seem strange that the mare's reproductive infection can affect the health of the foot. It is the fever associated with the infection that damages the laminae.

Twins. Twins occur more often in draft horses than in many light horse breeds. The mare is built to best produce one live foal.

Twins complicate the pregnancy, putting the mare and the foals at risk. Fortunately with the use of ultrasound, twins can be detected early. It is best to terminate one or both pregnancies.

MANAGING THE PREGNANT DRAFT MARE

It is important to the welfare of the mare and unborn foal that some extra management measures are taken during the mare's eleven-month gestation. Good nutrition, up-to-date vaccinations, and parasite control are the basics of good care.

Assuming the mare was in good condition when she was bred, her nutritional needs will not change for most of her pregnancy. The goal should be to keep her in a consistent condition. During the last trimester her needs will increase, but her greatest demand will be after the foal is born and is nursing. At that time more energy is needed to keep up the milk production.

One caution is to not feed endotoxic fescue grass or hay to the pregnant or lactating mare. Fescue can host a toxic fungus that causes a variety of problems in the pregnant mare including prolonged gestation, retained placenta, weak foals, and lack of milk production. Since the draft mare is already predisposed to many of these problems feeding toxic fescue will only compound the chances of trouble. The best remedy is prevention. Varieties of endophyte-free fescue have been developed and are safe to use. If in doubt have your county extension service examine the hay and test it for toxins. When planning pastures, plant one of the new varieties. Protein requirements for the pregnant mare are 8 to 12 percent. Once she is nursing her foal, that requirement increases to 16 percent. During the last trimester give the mare a free-choice calcium/phosphorous supplement. A recipe for this is: two parts salt, one part dicalcium phosphate, and one part feed-grade lime. Mix this and put it in a container where it will be available free choice to the mare at all times from the last third of her pregnancy until the foal is weaned. All the ingredients are available at farm supply or feed stores.

The mare should have plenty of fresh water and exercise.

CARE OF THE NEWBORN FOAL

Newborn draft foals tend to be less hardy and take longer to stand and nurse. For that reason it is important to keep a close watch on the mare as her time to foal draws near. A foal monitor is an ideal way to be alerted when the mare goes into labor. Record the time of breeding, to be able to estimate the foal's due date. Normal gestation is 335 to 345 days. If the mare is going to be relocated to have her foal, this should be done four to six weeks ahead of time. This gives the mare time to adjust and build immunity against any bacteria in the area and pass that on to the foal. As the pregnancy advances, the abdomen enlarges with the growth of the fetus. The mare will slow down her activity in the last period of her pregnancy, and in the last few weeks she will "drop," meaning the abdominal muscles have relaxed.

Knowing the signs of labor is important to being ready to call for assistance when necessary. There are three stages of labor. In the first stage the mare shows signs of nervous behavior. She will lie down and get back up repeatedly, switch her tail, begin sweating, urinate often, and may show signs similar to colic. This is because contractions have begun. At the end of stage one the water usually breaks. In the second stage, in normal birth, the front feet and nose appear first. If this is not the case, then the vet should be summoned right away. A malpresentation is easier to fix at this stage than later. Walk the mare until the vet arrives. In the third stage the fetus is expelled. This only takes about fifteen minutes. Again, if this stage takes longer call the vet. The placenta should be expelled within two hours of the foal's birth.

After making sure the foal is breathing, allow it to rest. Birth is hard work for both the mare and the foal. In a couple of minutes the normal foal will roll up on its chest. If it stays lying on its side, note that as abnormal and call the vet. The foal should also stand within at least one hour following birth. As soon as it stands up it will start looking for the mare's teats, and when it finds the right spot, it will begin nursing. Again, any variance from these normal activities is cause for concern and warrants a call to the vet.

Do not cut the unbiblical cord yourself, but let it break naturally when the mare stands. Drench the foal's unbiblical stub with iodine to prevent infection.

When the foal is born it does not have the ability to fight off infection or disease. The foal acquires this protection from antibodies produced by the mare and transferred by the first milk, or colostrum. The mare produces colostrum up to about twelve hours after giving birth. After twenty-four hours the foal gets no more antibodies from the milk.

WEANING THE FOAL

Weaning can be done as early as four months old if the foal has learned to eat grain and hay. By that age the mare is providing less and less nutrition to the foal through her milk. If there are two foals that can be weaned at the same time things will go easier. Put the foal or foals in a safe paddock or large box stall far enough away from the mares to be out of sight and hearing of each other if at all possible. Both the mare and foals should be settled down in their new environments in about one week.

CROSSBREEDING

Draft horses are often crossed with other breeds to customize a horse to fit a particular need or to eliminate an undesirable trait. The size, strength, and temperament of the draft horse make it a popular candidate for crossing with light horse breeds. The draft horse has also been crossed with the donkey to produce work mules. In addition, new draft breeds have been developed from crossbreeding.

"Pete" is a Belgian-Quarter Horse cross.

Many draft breed populations are small in numbers. In small populations there is always the risk that inbreeding will result in undesirable traits. Crossing out with another draft breed can produce hardier offspring. Another reason to crossbreed between draft breeds is to introduce a desired trait. One example of this is the Brabant's conversion to the modern Belgian. Today's Belgian is a taller, lighter-built horse with cleaner legs than its forefather, the Brabant, which was thick-bodied and had heavy feathering on its legs.

Crossing drafts with light horses is not new. In fact, many light breeds have their roots in the draft horse. Today's warmblood is the perfect example of combining the size, stamina, and even temperament of the draft horse with the refinement, speed, and athletic ability of

American Spotted Draft mare and foal grazing.

the hot-blooded Thoroughbred and Arabian. This type of horse was developed for sporting events like jumping, dressage, and eventing and has led to the development of sport breeds like the Hanoverian, Trakehner, and Oldenburg.

A draft crossed with a donkey will produce a hybrid, the mule. Usually the draft mare is bred to a Mammoth Jack to produce a large mule, but if a more refined mule is desired, the draft mare is bred to a smaller donkey. Mule fanciers believe mules to be much smarter than horses. That can be an advantage or disadvantage depending on how the mule is trained and handled. Mule fanciers claim the mule does not have as much flight instinct as horses, but will be more inclined to stop and evaluate a problem rather than jump and run. The mule also has a keen sense of preservation and will not be forced into what it considers a dangerous situation. Some judge this personality trait as stubbornness, but others say it's just plain good sense.

Whatever direction and goal the breeder has, there is nothing that compares to the feeling a breeder gets when he or she sees their mare's first foal emerge, and all is well with mama and baby. It is truly a miracle in action.

RESOURCES

BREEDS

American Brabant Association
2331 Oak Dr.
Ijamsville, MD 21754
301-631-2222
www.ruralheritage.com/brabant/index.htm

American Cream Draft Horse Association
193 Crossover Rd.
Bennington, VT 05201
802-447-7612
www.acdha.org

American Haflinger Registry
1686 East Waterloo Rd.
Akron, OH 44306-4103
330-784-0000
http://haflingerhorse.com

American Shire Horse Association
Pamela Correll
1211 Hill Harrell Rd.
Effingham, SC 29541
www.shirehorse.org

American Suffolk Association
Mary Margaret M. Read
4240 Goehring Rd.
Ledbetter, TX 78946-5004
www.suffolkpunch.com

Belgian Draft Horse Corporation of America
PO Box 335
Wabash, IN 46992
www.belgiancorp.com

Clydesdale Breeders of America
17346 Kelley Rd.
Pecatonia, IL 61063
815-247-8780
http://clydesusa.com

Draft Cross Breeders and Owners
PO Box 50275
Indianapolis, IN 42650
www.draftcrossbreedersandowners.com

North American Spotted Draft Horse Association
17420 US Hwy 20
Goshen, IN 46528
www.nasdha.net

Norwegian Fjord Horse Registry
1203 Appian Dr.
Webster, NY 14580
585-872-4114
www.nfhr.com

Percheron Horse Association of America
PO Box 141
10330 Quaker Rd.
Fredericktown, OH 43019
740-694-3602
www.percheronhorse.org

The Pinto Draft Registry, Inc.
PO Box 738
Estancia, NM 87016
505-384-1000
www.pinto-draft-registry.com

FOUNDATIONS

Healing Harvest Forest Foundation
Jason Rutledge, President
8014 Bear Ridge Rd. SE
Copper Hill, VA 24079
540-651-6355
Rutledge@swva.net

ORGANIZATIONS AND EVENTS

The Carriage Association of America
3915 Jay Trump Rd.
Lexington, KY 40511
859-231-0971
www.caaonline.com

Eastern Draft Horse Association
Jody Whipple
103 Anthony Rd.
North Stonington, CT 06359
www.easterndrafthorse.com

Equine Assisted Growth and Learning Association (EAGALA)
PO Box 993
Santaquin, UT 84655
877-858-4600
www.eagala.org/

North Carolina Draft and
Mule Association
1256 Longest Acres Rd.
Snow Camp, NC 27349

Southeast Old Threshers' Reunion
1366 Jim Elliot Rd.
Denton, NC 27239
336-859-2755
www.threshers.com

PHOTOGRAPHER

Roey Yohai, NYC Photographer
www.rohai.com

PUBLICATIONS

The Draft Horse Journal
PO Box 670
2700 Fifth Ave.
Waverly, IA 50677
319-352-4046
www.drafthorsejournal.com

Rural Heritage
281 Dean Ridge Ln.
Gainesboro, TN 38562-5039
www.rualheritage.com

Small Farmers Journal
PO Box 1627
Sisters, OR 97759-1627
1-800-876-2893
www.smallfarmersjournal.com

GLOSSARY

Anterior enteritis – Inflammation of the intestines.

Antibodies – Immunizing agent in the horse's body that fights disease.

Artificial insemination – Method of breeding in which the semen is collected from the stallion and injected into the uterus of the mare.

Auction – A sale in which the horse is sold to the highest bidder.

Azoturia, Monday morning disease – A metabolic disorder in which large amounts of lactic acid accumulate in the muscles and destroy muscle cells, releasing myoglobin into the system. This causes stiffness of the muscles after exercise.

Banamine – An anti-inflammatory drug.

Bay – Brown or red horse with black mane and tail, and black on the lower legs.

Belly band/stud belt – A surcingle, which is fitted around the girth area, with a strap running from the bit to the right side of the band. Used on Clydesdale and Shire stallions when shown in-hand.

Big head disease – A condition caused by an imbalance of calcium and phosphorous in the diet. Usually occurs in growing horses, causes limb deformities, lameness, and/or enlarged head.

Big Hitch – Multi-horse hitch.

Black Horse of Flanders – The stocky, draft-type wild horse of Western Europe that was present at the time of the Roman Invasion. It is considered the "father of all draft horses."

Boston Match – A team of horses that are different colors and/or breeds.

Box stall – A stall large enough for a horse to move around freely and lie down.

Braiding bench – A bench used to stand on while braiding a horse's mane. Allows the groom to work while looking down on the mane.

Breed character – Those characteristics in a horse that identify it with a certain breed.

Carrier – A horse that can transmit certain diseases to another horse without showing symptoms of the disease itself.

Chestnut – A reddish brown horse. The mane and tail can vary from the same color as the body to blonde or flaxen.

Chronic disease – A disease that is recurrent or continues a long time.

Coggins test – A blood test used to detect equine infectious anemia.

Cold-blooded – A horse with draft breeding, called cold-blooded because of the northern European countries of their origin.

Colic – Abdominal pain.

Colostrum – A mare's first milk. It contains antibodies that provide immunity against many diseases for the foal.

Concentrate – Food high in energy-producing carbohydrates and fats.

Conestoga Horse – A type of horse bred in the Conestoga Valley of Pennsylvania to pull the Conestoga wagons of that region in the 19th century.

Conformation – The way a horse is built.

Coronary band – Sensitive skin tissue at the top of the hoof.

Crossbreeding – Breeding horses of two different breeds or bloodlines.

Croup – The top line of the hindquarter.

Dental bumps – Bumps visible from the exterior of the lower jaw, caused by retained dental caps.

Dental caps – Baby teeth that remain attached after adult teeth erupt.

Dental hooks – Sharp edges on the molars formed from uneven wear.

Deworm – To administer a medication that kills internal parasites.

Docked tail – A tail that has been shortened by surgical means.

Draft horse – A heavy horse used for work.

Dynamometer – A machine that measures the weight a horse can pull.

Dystocia – A difficult birth.

Equine encephalomyelitis – Also known as sleeping sickness; an inflammation of the brain caused by a virus. The virus is transmitted by biting insects.

Equine Infectious Anemia (EIA) – A viral disease which affects the immune system. It is transmitted from horse to horse by biting insects or contaminated needles.

Equine polysaccharide storage myopathy (EPSM) – A condition found in draft horses in which glycogen and glycogen related compounds are stored in the muscles instead of being used as energy. This leads to various symptoms including a stiff gait, muscle cramps, shivers, azoturia, wasting away of muscles, and weakness. A low-carbohydrate, high-fat diet is the best prevention.

Feathering – Long hair which grows on the lower part of the horse's legs.

Fescue – A cool season grass used for pasture and hay production.

Flaxen – Blonde hair of the mane and tail.

Foal monitor – An electronic or mechanical device that sounds an alarm when a mare goes into labor, usually is activated when the mare lies down flat, as it usually does when in labor.

Forage – Leafy feedstuff including pasture, hay, and silage.

Forearm – Upper part of the front limb of the horse.

Founder – A crippling condition caused by laminitis, an inflammation of the laminae of the foot.

Gaskin – The large muscle between the hip and hock of the hind leg.

Gestation – Period of time from conception until the birth of a foal.

Grease heel, mud fever, scratches – Dermatitis of the skin on the back of the pastern, which causes inflammation and scabbing of the area.

Gymkhana – A horse event consisting of various games played while on horseback. Some examples are barrel racing, keyhole race, and relay races.

Header – An assistant in driving classes who stands at the head of the horse during lineup to steady the horse if it becomes nervous.

Hitch – Horse(s) and the vehicle it/they pull.

Horse pull – A contest that tests the horses' ability to pull heavy weight.

Hyperthyroidism – See Big Head Disease.

Immunity – Protection by antibodies against certain diseases.

In-hand class – Classes in a horse show in where a handler leads the horse.

Internal parasite – Organisms that that live and feed inside the body of the horse. Examples are round worms, bots, and pinworms.

Jutland Horse – A draft horse that originated in Denmark's Jutland Peninsula, dating back to the Middle Ages. It is medium sized, chestnut with flaxen mane and tail, heavy feathering on its legs, with a quick and free way of going.

Keratin – Protein that makes up hair, hooves, and other horny tissue.

Laminitis – See founder.

Lead-line class – Class in a horse show in which a small child rides a horse that is being led by an adult.

Log skidding – Pulling logs out of the woods.

Malpresentation – A fetus that is moving through the birth canal in an abnormal position, such as with its head turned back or hindquarters first (breech). The front feet and nose should appear first in a normal presentation.

Methionine – An essential amino acid needed to produce keratin.

Novice – An inexperienced horse person.

Paddling – A gait defect in which the front feet swing outward. Caused by toed-in conformation. This usually results in interference.

Paleolithic – Pertaining to the Old Stone Age.

Pastern – That part of the leg between the hoof and fetlock.

Pinto – A horse with patches of color with white.

Placenta – The organ that joins the fetus to the mare's uterus.

Pleasure horse – A horse used for personal recreation and companionship.

Pre-purchase vet exam – An examination done on a horse by a veterinarian before a prospective buyer closes the deal.

Rabies – An infectious disease of the central nervous system, usually fatal. It can be transmitted from one mammal species to another.

Roached back – The back is convex and lacks flexibility.

Roached mane – A mane that is shaved completely off.

Roan – A horse whose coat has an evenly distributed mixture of white and dark hairs from birth.

Roman nosed – A horse whose profile is convex.

Scotch bottoms – A shoe with edges that slope out from top to bottom with the angle of the hoofwall. They make the hoof appear bigger, and in fact give the bottom more surface. Are used on show horses.

Shivers – A chronic neuromuscular disease. Symptoms are spasms of the hindquarter, jerking of the tail, and inability to back up.

Show stick – A short stick, about 18 inches, used to cue a draft horse when showing in-hand.

Showmanship – An in-hand class in which the handler's proficiency in showing the horse is being judged.

Sport horse – Horses bred for competition in sporting events like jumping, dressage, and eventing. Usually have warmblood or other draft and light horse bloodlines.

Stone boat – A sled that hold the weights for a horse pulling contest.

Strangles – A very contagious bacterial disease. Symptoms include high fever, nasal discharge, swollen lymph glands, coughing, and difficulty swallowing.

Supplements – Substances like vitamins, minerals, or fats added to a horse's feed ration.

Surcingle – Web or leather strap that fits around a horse's girth area.

Tetanus – Caused by the anaerobic bacterium *Clostridium tetani*. Usually fatal.

Throat latch – The part of the horse where the head and neck come together. The strap on a bridle or halter that goes across the throat latch to keep the bridle or halter from coming off.

Thrush – A disease of the foot cause by anaerobic bacteria. Signs are a thick, black discharge and foul odor. Good hygiene and dry environment are the best deterrents.

Tie stall – A narrow stall in which the horse is tied.

Top line – The top of the horse when viewed from the side.

Toxic shock – A severe bacterial infection, usually fatal.

Trailer/whipper – An assistant that helps the handler by moving from behind the horse to encourage the horse to move forward.

Umbilical cord – Tissue that attaches the blood vessels from the placenta to the foal.

Umbilical stump – Tissue remaining attached to the foal after the umbilical cord breaks away.

Unsoundness – An injury or flaw that prevents a horse from being useful.

Ventral edema – Accumulation of fluid in the lower part of the belly surface.

Warmblood – A type of horse resulting from cross-breeding draft horses with Thoroughbreds or Arabians.

Weaning – Separating foals and their dams so that the foals are no longer nursing.

West Nile – A virus that causes inflammation of the brain. It is spread to horses and other creatures by mosquito bites and can cause death.

Wheel Position/wheel horse/wheel team – The horses in a hitch positioned directly in front of the vehicle.

Winging – A gait defect in which the front feet swing inward. Caused by toed-out conformation of the foot.

Wolf teeth – Small teeth located in front of the upper premolars.

BIBLIOGRAPHY

BOOKS

Ensminger, M E. *Horses and Horsemanship*. 5th ed. Danville, Illinois: The Interstate Printers and Publishers, Inc, 1977.

Evans, J. Warren. *Horses*. 1st ed. San Francisco, CA: WH Freeman and Company, 1981.

Harris, Moira C. *America's Horses*. 1st ed. Guilford, Connecticut: The Lyons Press, 2003.

Mischka, Robert A. *It's Showtime! A Beginner's Guide to Showing Draft Horses*. 1st ed. Whitewater, Wisconsin: Heart Prairie Press, 1998.

Shideler, R K., and J L. Voss. *Management of the Pregnant Mare and Newborn Foal*. 1st ed. Fort Collins, CO: Animal Reproduction Laboratory, Colorado State University, 1984.

Telleen, Maurice. *The Draft Horse Primer*. 1st ed. Emmaus, PA: Rodale, 1977.

Wagoner, Don M., and M M. Vale, DMV. *The Illustrated Veterinary Encyclopedia for Horsemen*. 2nd ed. Tyler, Texas: Equine Research Publications, 1977.

PAMPHLETS

Horse Handbook, Housing and Equipment. Fort Collins, CO: Colorado State University Cooperative Extension Service, 1995.

ARTICLES

Feld, Ellen. "The Fencing Question." *Stable Management Magazine*, Aug. 2005: 37.

"Original Horsepower." *North Carolina Farm Bureau*, May 2006: 8-9.

Schmidt, Vicki. "Fire Horses." *Rural Heritage*, Autumn 2005: 74-75.

"The Way I See It: The Danger of Single Trait Over-Selection," *Western Horseman*, August 1998: 120-124.

"The World's Largest Horse." *The Draft Horse Journal*, Spring 1994: 84-85.

"What is This Urine Business All About?" *The Draft Horse Journal*, Autumn 1993: 26-29.

WEB SITES

Amanda and Craig, "The Role of the Horse in World War One," *W.W.1 Horse.* **http://www.geocities.com/wwihorse** (accessed May 30, 2006).

"The American Belgian," *Stateline Tack.* **http://www.statelinetack.com/global/articles/article_detail. jsp?CONTENT%3C%3Ecnt_id=10134198673311331&FO LDER%3C%3Efolder_id=9852723696504112&N=231** (accessed June 15, 2006).

"American Brabant Association," *Rural Heritage*, April 18, 2006, **www.ruralheritage.com/brabant** (accessed June 28, 2006).

American Shire Horse Association. **www.shirehorse.org** (accessed April 27, 2006).

Anderson, Bruce. *Nature's View.* **http://www.naturesview1.org** (accessed June 17, 2006).

"Animal Power," Small Farmers Journal. 2001. **http://www.smallfarmersjournal.com** (accessed June 24, 2006).

"The Big E – Judging a Hitch," *The Big E – Eastern States Expo.* 2006. **http://www.thebige.com/horseshow/draft/hs_draft_ judging.html** (accessed June 24, 2006).

Boin, Sonia. "Horse Therapy for War Amputees," *Int'l Fund for Horses*. February 25, 2006. http://www.fund4horses.org/info.php?id=680 (accessed July 24, 2006).

"A Brief History of the Breed," *Belgian Draft Horse Corporation of America*. 2004. www.belgiancorp.com/files/history1.html (accessed June 28, 2006).

Brown, Eric W."How to Sell or Show a Draft Horse," *North American Spotted Draft Horse Association*. 2004. http://www.nasdha.net/LearningCenter/showing.htm (accessed May 12, 2006).

Christie, Julie L., Caroline J. Hewson, Christopher B. Riley, Mary A. McNiven, Ian R. Dohoo, and Luis A. Bate. "Demographics, Management, and Welfare of Nonracing Horses in Prince Edward Island," *The Canadian Veterinarian Journal*. Dec. 2004. http://www.pubmedcentral.nih.gov/articlerender.fcgi?artid=554751 (accessed May 18, 2006).

"Conestoga Wagons," *Ulster American Folk Park*. http://www.folkpark.com/collections/the_journey/conestoga_wagons (accessed June 28, 2006).

DiVita, Lee J. "Veterinary, equine community dispel accusations against the pregnant mare urine industry," *AVMA Journal*. April 15, 2002. http://www.avma.org/onlnews/javma/apr02/s041502d.asp (accessed July 2, 2006).

"Draft Breeds," *Draft Horse Resource*. September 28, 2004. www.draftresource.com/Draft_breeds.html (accessed June 30, 2006).

"Draft Horse Showmanship," Government of Nova Scotia Canada. 2006. http://www.gov.ns.ca/nsaf/4h/show/draftshow.shtml (accessed 2006).

Ellingson, J. and L. Coates-Markle, "Managing Your Pregnant

Mare and Her Foal," Oregon State University. April 1996.
http://extension.oregonstate.edu/catalog/html/ec/ec147
6/#anchor1415691 (accessed June 25, 2006).

English, Martin, DVM, "Equine Disease Update," *Clydesdale
Breeders of the USA*. 2002. http://clydesusa.com/lh46_
Equine_diseases_update.htm (accessed May 18, 2006).

"Equine Pregnancy," *LSU School of Veterinary Medicine*. 2006.
http://www.vetmed.lsu.edu/eiltslotus/theriogenology-
5361/equine%20pregnancy_2.htm (accessed June 25, 2006).

Gibson, Emily (ed) "Halflinger Breed Information," *Haflinger Horses*.
www.haflingerhorses.com/info.htm (accessed June 30, 2006).

Grandin, Temple, (ed) "Genetics and the Behavior of Domestic
Animals," *Dr. Temple Grandin's Web Page*, Colorado State
University, Fort Collins, CO.
http://www.grandin.com/inc/genetics.bk.html
(accessed June 24, 2006).

Hard, Touchstone B. "Following the Plow," *Mother Earth News*.
March/April 1974.
http://www.motherearthnews.com/Livestock_and_Farm-
ing/ 1974_March_April/Following_the_Plow
(accessed May 18, 2006).

Hynes, James W. and James R. Lindner. "Lessons from the Draft
Horse Industry in East Texas," *Journal of Extension*. April 2006.
http://www.joe.org/joe/2006april/rb3.shtml
(accessed May 21, 2006).

Illingworth, Clare and Kristy Nudds. "Skin Detectives,"
University of Guelph Research News. October 19, 2002.
http://www.uoguelph.ca/research/news/articles/2002/
skin_detectives.shtml (accessed June 22, 2006).

"JEB Facts," *Belgian Draft Horse Corporation of America*.
http://www.belgiancorp.com/files/jeb1.html
(accessed May 18, 2006).

Kline, Robert, Shea Porr, and John Cardina, "Horse Nutrition,"
The Ohio State University.
http://ohioline.osu.edu/b762/index.html
(accessed June 19, 2006).

Merrick, Lisa. "How to Braid Draft Horse Manes and Tails,"
Draft Horse Resource. 2001.
http://www.draftresource.com/Draft_Braids.html
(accessed April 24, 2006).

North American Spotted Draft Horse Association. 2005.
www.nasdha.net (accessed June 24, 2006).

"Percheron History," Breeds of Livestock, Oklahoma State
University. September 6, 1999.
www.ansi.okstate.edu/breeds/horses/percheron/index.htm
(accessed June 24, 2006).

Percheron Horse Association of America. 2001.
www.percheronhorse.org
(accessed May 23, 2006).

Perkins, N R., T L. Blanchard, J Orsini, and W R. Threlfall.
"Prevalence of Fetal Maldispositions in Equine Referral Hospital Dystocias." **Pub Med**. National Library of Medicine. 2006.
http://www.ncbi.nlm.nih.gov/entrez/query.fcgi?cmd=
Retrieve&db=PubMed&list_uids=9104559&dopt=Abstract
(accessed June 25, 2006)

Pinto Draft Registry. 2005.
www.pinto-draft-registry.com (Accessed May 07, 2006)

"PMU Foals," *Spring Hill Rescue.* 2006.
http://www.springhillrescue.com/pmu.shtml#Foals,
(accessed June 13, 2006).

Pope, Elizabeth. "Not Your Average Team," *Vermont Quarterly
Online Magazine.* 2000.
http://universitycommunications.uvm.edu/vq/VQSPRIN
G00/team.html (accessed June 24, 2006).

Pycock, Jonathan B. Ph.D., D.E.S.M., M.R.C.V.S. "Late Term
Pregnancy Problems in the Mare –Ventral Ruptures," *Equine
Reproduction.* April 2003.
http://www.equine-reproduction.com/articles/rupture.shtml
(accessed June 26, 2006).

Sandor, Dan. *Brigadier's Law.* 2006.
http://www.brigadierslaw.ca
(accessed August 11, 2006).

Santamaria, Sue, "Fescue Toxicosis in Pregnant Mares,"
Purdue University School of Veterinary Medicine. 2001.
www.vet.purdue.edu/horses/Fescue.htm
(accessed June 27, 2006).

"Tips," *Utopia Percherons.* 2004.
www.utopiapercherons.com (accessed April 27, 2006).

Valberg, Stephanie DVM PhD Dip. ACVIM, and John Baird
BVSc. PhD "Shivers," *University of Minnesota, Neuromuscular
Diagnostic Laboratory.* 2005.
**http://academic-server.cvm.umn.edu/neuromuscularlab/
Shivers.htm**
(accessed May 18, 2006).

Valentine, Beth A. DVM, PhD, "EPMS—Muscle Disease in Draft
Horses, Rural Heritage Vet Clinic," *Rural Heritage,* April 5,
2006.
http://www.ruralheritage.com/vet_clinic/epsm.htm
(accessed June 18, 2006).

Valentine, Beth A. DVM, PhD, "Feeding Draft Horses:
The EPSM Diet," *Equus Caballus Magazine.* 2004.
http://www.ecmagazine.net/ecfall05/FeedingDrafts.htm
(accessed June 17, 2006).

PERSONAL INTERVIEWS

Al Boykin, 2006

Amy Snyder, 2006

Barry D. Leonard, 2006

Bruce Anderson, 2006

C.B. Daughtridge, 2006

Craig Miron, e-mail message to author, 2006

Denise Pullis, e-mail message to author, 2006

Frankie Faithful, 2006

Hannah K. Johnson, e-mail message to author, 2006

Hope Griffis, e-mail message to author, 2006

Jason Rutledge, e-mail message to author, 2006

Jennifer Tredway, e-mail message to author, 2006

Jimmy Dozier, 2006

Kim Jones, e-mail message to author, 2006

Lisa Miller, 2006

Michele Bright, e-mail message to author, 2006

Neil Dimmock, e-mail message to author, 2006

Robert L. Garner, 2006

Rosanna L. White, 2006

Roxanne Thrower, e-mail message to author, 2006

Sarah Featherstone, e-mail message to author, 2006

Steve Wisnieski, e-mail message to author, 2006

Susan Bothern, e-mail message to author, 2006

INDEX